THE PEANUTS GUIDE
TO PIZZA, PARTIES, PEANUT BUTTER, AND S'MORE

A JUMBO ACTIVITY BOOK

BASED ON THE COMIC STRIP BY CHARLES M. SCHULZ

ACTIVITIES BY ELIZABETH BENNETT

SCHOLASTIC INC.

New York Toronto London Auckland Sydney Mexico City
New Delhi Hong Kong Buenos Aires

P9-CRM-712

Copyright © 2003 United Feature Syndicate, Inc.
All rights reserved. PEANUTS is a registered trademark of United Feature Syndicate, Inc.
PEANUTS © United Feature Syndicate, Inc.
www.snoopy.com
Based on the PEANUTS ® comic strips by Charles M. Schulz.

ISBN: 0-439-46822-1

Published by Scholastic Inc. All rights reserved.
SCHOLASTIC and associated logos are trademarks and/or registered trademarks of Scholastic Inc.

Designed by Julie Mullarkey-Gnoy
Activities illustrated by Yancey Labat
Cover illustration by Pete and Nick LoBianco

12 11 10 9 8 7 6 5 4 3 2 1   3 4 5 6 7 8/0

Printed in the U.S.A.

First Scholastic printing, February 2003

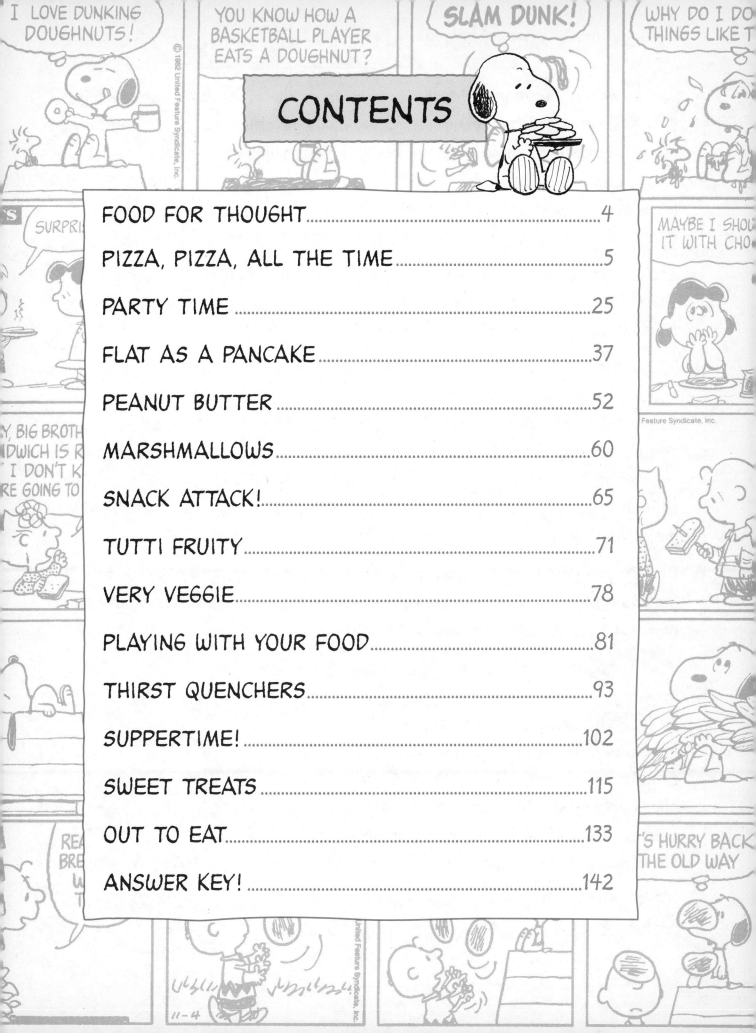

CONTENTS

FOOD FOR THOUGHT 4

PIZZA, PIZZA, ALL THE TIME 5

PARTY TIME 25

FLAT AS A PANCAKE 37

PEANUT BUTTER 52

MARSHMALLOWS 60

SNACK ATTACK! 65

TUTTI FRUITY 71

VERY VEGGIE 78

PLAYING WITH YOUR FOOD 81

THIRST QUENCHERS 93

SUPPERTIME! 102

SWEET TREATS 115

OUT TO EAT 133

ANSWER KEY! 142

FOOD FOR THOUGHT

For nearly 50 years, Charles Schulz drew the PEANUTS comic strip. And from the beginning, Charlie Brown's lovable dog Snoopy had a huge appetite. Nothing makes Snoopy happier than suppertime. Whether it's pizza, cookies, or snacks at a pool party in Woodstock's birdbath, Snoopy loves to eat! And he's not the only one! Take Peppermint Patty, for example. What would lunchtime be like without her weird choices?

Ice cream sundaes, hot chocolate, peanut butter, lemonade—*The Peanuts Guide to Pizza, Parties, Peanut Butter, and S'more*, featuring Charlie Brown, Snoopy, and the rest of the Peanuts Gang, has it all!

Enjoy the comic strips, try the delicious recipes, make crafts out of yummy foods like peanut butter and marshmallows, challenge yourself with the puzzles, and get some great new party ideas. If you're stumped on one of the puzzles (or want to find out just how good you are at solving them), check the Answer Key at the back of the book. This jumbo activity book is sure to keep you busy for hours. But be careful, because it might also make you hungry!

Before you get started, you'll want to gather some supplies, like a few pencils and an eraser. For the food activities, you'll need cooking utensils and ingredients, and a grown-up to help you.

P.S. Throughout this book, you'll notice that drawings of the PEANUTS characters don't all look the same. That's because of the incredibly long length of time that Charles Schulz was drawing the PEANUTS strip—almost half a century! Imagine how much *your* drawing style would change if you were to draw for that much time!

P.P.S. And don't forget, since this is an activity book, it's OKAY to write in this book!

PIZZA, PIZZA, ALL THE TIME

NOW SNOOPY CAN MAKE HIS OWN PIE

(5-12-59)

DO-IT-YOURSELF PIZZA

WHAT YOU NEED: (makes 1 large pie, 8-10 slices)

1 large, ready-made pizza crust (like a Boboli)

2 cups tomato sauce

3 cups grated mozzarella cheese

Parmesan cheese

toppings (see list below)

You'll also need a round or rectangular baking pan (like a cookie sheet), a large spoon, measuring cups and spoons, and an adult to help you.

WHAT YOU DO:

1. Preheat the oven to 375°F.

2. Place the pizza crust on the large round or rectangular baking pan.

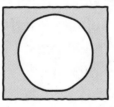

3. Use the large spoon to spread the tomato sauce over the crust.

4. Cover the sauce with the mozzarella cheese. Add any other toppings, and sprinkle some Parmesan cheese on top.

5. Bake for 16-18 minutes. Then remove it from the oven and let it cool for a few minutes.

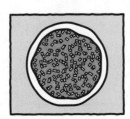

6. Cut into slices and serve!

TOPPING IDEAS:

4 plum tomatoes, sliced

1 cup fresh mushrooms, sliced

1 cup zucchini, sliced

½ cup sliced ham

1 cup spinach, chopped

1 cup goat cheese

3 cups grated cheddar cheese

8 ounces pepperoni, sliced

1 cup cooked, chopped, boneless chicken breast

1 red or green pepper, sliced

½ cup pitted black olives, sliced

chopped fresh herbs like parsley, basil, oregano

1 cup pineapple chunks

It's worth overcoming your fears when the reward is pizza! What do you like on your pies? Find all of the toppings listed in the word box below in the word search puzzle on the next page. The answers can be found forward, backward, up, down, and diagonally.

WORD BOX

ANCHOVIES	EGGPLANT	GARLIC	BACON
MEATBALLS	HAM	HERBS	PEPPERONI
MUSHROOMS	SAUSAGE	TOMATO	ONIONS
BROCCOLI	PEPPERS	SALAMI	SPINACH
CHEESE	SHRIMP	OLIVES	PESTO
OREGANO	CLAMS		

I	L	O	C	C	O	R	B	A	C	O	N	O
M	S	S	R	E	P	P	E	P	H	H	E	R
E	G	G	P	L	A	N	T	S	E	S	C	E
A	A	P	E	N	D	E	F	P	E	A	S	G
T	I	M	P	E	S	T	O	I	S	L	M	A
B	N	I	P	I	T	T	V	N	E	A	O	N
A	C	R	E	E	A	O	L	A	Y	M	O	O
L	I	H	R	M	H	N	M	C	A	I	R	H
L	L	S	O	C	A	I	K	H	E	A	H	E
S	R	T	N	L	O	O	L	I	V	E	S	R
T	A	A	I	O	F	N	D	O	U	G	U	B
E	G	A	S	U	A	S	H	C	L	A	M	S

Now write the leftover letters (the ones that aren't circled) in the order that they appear, left to right, row by row, on the lines below to answer this riddle:

Why would Lucy want to own her own pizza restaurant?

_____

_____

HAVE A SLICE!

Snoopy has a huge appetite for pizza!

(12-26-59)

Snoopy loves pizza. When he says he can eat a whole pizza "without batting a lip," he means he could easily eat that much pizza. "Without batting a lip" is a play on the expression "without batting an eye," which means to do something calmly and naturally, as if it's a habit.

There are six 24-inch pizza pies pictured below. Each pie is sliced differently—one pie has four slices, one pie has six, one has eight, one has 10, one has 12, and another has 14. For each picture, count the number of slices Snoopy would eat if he ate only half a pie and write that number in the box below each one.

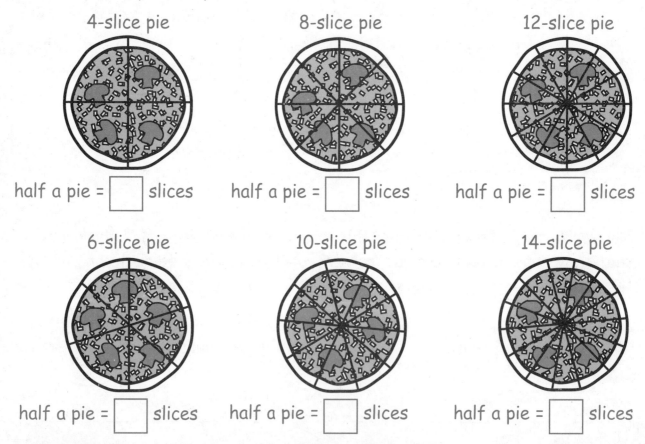

4-slice pie   8-slice pie   12-slice pie

half a pie = ☐ slices   half a pie = ☐ slices   half a pie = ☐ slices

6-slice pie   10-slice pie   14-slice pie

half a pie = ☐ slices   half a pie = ☐ slices   half a pie = ☐ slices

BONUS QUESTION: The pizza with which number of slices—4, 6, 8, 10, 12, or 14— would fill Snoopy up the most?

8

MINI PIZZA

Snoopy's midnight snack!

(8-12-69)

Here's an easy recipe for a mini pizza that you can make any time, even at midnight!

ENGLISH MUFFIN MINI PIZZA

(makes 1 mini pizza)

WHAT YOU NEED:

1 tablespoon tomato sauce

½ english muffin

1 tablespoon grated
   mozzarella cheese

assorted toppings,
such as bell pepper,
black olives,
or pepperoni

You'll also need a spoon and a toaster oven or a regular oven.

WHAT YOU DO:

1. Spread the tomato sauce on the english muffin half.

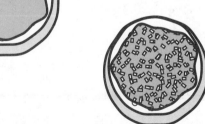

2. Cover the sauce with the cheese and any toppings you like.

3. Heat the mini pizza in the toaster oven or oven broiler for 3-5 minutes, until the cheese is melted.

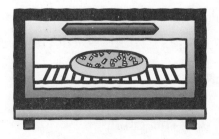

4. Enjoy!

WORLD RECORD PIZZA EATER

How many pizzas do you think you could eat all at one time?

(1-2-76)

Snoopy tried to break the world record for eating the most pizzas.
How do you think Snoopy would feel if he tried to eat one of these
record-breaking foods from the *Guinness Book of World Records*?

WORLD'S BIGGEST PIZZA

122' 8" in diameter

Norwood Hypermarket

Norwood, South Africa

December 8, 1990

WORLD'S BIGGEST PANCAKE

49' 3" in diameter

1 inch deep

Greater Manchester, England

April 2, 1996

WORLD'S BIGGEST COOKIE

81' 8" in diameter

Christchurch, New Zealand

April 2, 1996

WORLD'S LONGEST NOODLE

181' long

Pasir Panjung Family Fun Day

Singapore

May 30, 1999

(' is the symbol for feet and " is the symbol for inches.
Diameter is how far across it is from one side of a circle to the other side.)

If you could hold a world record for making the biggest
or longest food, what food would it be?

World's Biggest or Longest _____

Check out the Guinness Book of World Records
or http://www.guinnessworldrecords.com to find out about other world records.

PIZZA SURPRISE

Where's pizza going to turn up next?

(9-1-91)

What sports do you like to play?
Can you change this comic strip to show your favorite sport?
For example, you could have a pizza basketball,
pepperoni swim goggles, or a cheesy pizza tennis racquet.
Draw your pizza sport ideas below.

PIZZA: MORNING, NOON, AND NIGHT

(1-27-58)

Tired of pizza for lunch every day? How about pizza for dessert instead? Try a Chocolate Cookie Pizza! Or go for a double dose of Snoopy's favorite food: have a regular pizza for lunch and this sweet pizza for dessert!

CHOCOLATE COOKIE PIZZA

(makes 1 large pie)

PIZZA CRUST

> ### WHAT YOU NEED:
>
> butter to grease the pan
>
> 1 egg
>
> ¼ cup granulated (white) sugar
>
> ½ cup packed brown sugar
>
> ½ cup (1 stick) butter or margarine
>
> 1 teaspoon vanilla extract
>
> 1¼ cups flour
>
> ½ teaspoon baking soda

You'll also need a cookie sheet (or pizza pan), a large bowl, a large mixing spoon, measuring cups and spoons, and an adult to help you.

WHAT YOU DO:

1. Preheat the oven to 350°F. Grease the cookie sheet or pizza pan with butter.

2. In the large bowl, mix the egg, brown sugar, white sugar, butter, and vanilla with the large mixing spoon.

3. Add the flour and baking soda. Stir with the spoon until everything is mixed (the dough will be stiff).

4. Pat the dough into a flat disk on the cookie sheet or pizza pan.

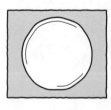

5. Bake for 15 minutes.

6. Let the crust cool while you prepare the sauce.

12

CHOCOLATE COOKIE PIZZA SAUCE

WHAT YOU NEED:

1 bag (6 oz.) semisweet chocolate chips

2 tablespoons butter or margarine

3 tablespoons milk

1 cup powdered sugar

You'll also need a small saucepan and a wooden spoon.

WHAT YOU DO:

1. Put the chocolate chips, butter, and milk in the saucepan. Cook over a low heat, stirring with the wooden spoon, until the chocolate is melted.

2. Add the powdered sugar and stir until smooth.

3. Remove the saucepan from the heat and turn off the stove.

4. Use the spoon to spread the sauce over your cooled "pizza crust."

5. You can make your chocolate cookie pizza look like a real pizza by sprinkling it with "cheese" and other "toppings" listed below.

6. Cut into slices and enjoy!

TOPPING IDEAS:

shredded coconut for "cheese"

red fruit leather cut into circles for "pepperoni"

green gumdrops for "green bell peppers"

black gumdrops for "olives"

Panel 1: WHY DO I DO IT?

Panel 2: WHY DO I EAT THINGS LIKE THAT?

Panel 3: NOW I FEEL TERRIBLE.. I NEVER LEARN...

Panel 4: PIZZA A LA MODE

(9-20-86)

ANOTHER IDEA: You can also spread soft vanilla ice cream on your pizza and top it with strawberries—it'll look like mozzarella with tomatoes!

PIZZA MATH

Night Night!

Snoopy ate five pizzas before going to bed. That's A LOT of pizza!

One of Snoopy's pizzas had eight slices.

Two of Snoopy's pizzas had 10 slices each.

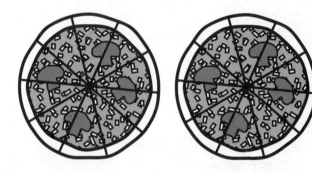

Two of Snoopy's pizzas had six slices each.

How many slices of pizza did Snoopy eat altogether?

RAINY PIZZA DAYS

What does Snoopy think about the rain?

Put the scrambled words below in the correct order to find out.

COOL PIZZA

YOUR DOWN

TENDS TO IT

Write the unscrambled sentence here:

_____

_____

_____

COLORFUL EXPRESSIONS

What does Snoopy really mean?

(1-22-80)

When Snoopy says that "the early bird gets the worm," he is trying to tell Woodstock that the earlier you start something, the more you get done. Expressions like this—words grouped together to mean something different than what they actually say—are called idioms. That is, they're sentences with hidden meanings! See if you can guess the real meaning of each idiom below.

1 When you say to a friend, "DON'T CRY OVER SPILLED MILK," you mean:

a) you shouldn't cry when you're near a puddle of milk because your tears will make your vision blurry and you might slip and fall.

b) if you let your tears fall into a pool of milk, it will only make the puddle bigger.

c) it's too late to worry about a mistake you made.

2 If your mom "BRINGS HOME THE BACON," she:

a) leads a pig home on a leash.

b) buys bacon at the grocery store.

c) earns money for the household.

3 "THAT'S A TOUGH NUT TO CRACK" means:

a) the task is difficult to accomplish.

b) the coconut shell is very hard.

c) you can't crack open a walnut because you don't have a nutcracker.

4 If someone "BUTTERS YOU UP," he:

a) spreads butter on your hands.

b) acts extra nice to try to get you to do something he wants you to do.

c) puts butter on your sandwich.

⑤ If your friend is "IN A JAM," she:

a) spilled jelly all over the floor.

b) is stuck in traffic.

c) got herself into some kind of trouble.

⑥ "YOU HAVE ANTS IN YOUR PANTS" means:

a) your pants are so dirty that they're full of bugs.

b) you are restless.

c) you like to spend time outside (and close to nature).

⑦ If you're "USING YOUR NOODLE," you are:

a) thinking well.

b) hitting someone with a wet noodle.

c) making a necklace out of macaroni.

⑧ If you "PULL SOMEONE'S LEG," you are:

a) in a wrestling match or a fight.

b) teasing someone by telling them an exaggerated story.

c) helping someone stretch his legs.

⑨ If your sister "PUTS HER FOOT DOWN," she is:

a) learning to walk.

b) stepping on a bug.

c) being firm about something.

⑩ If you do your homework at "THE ELEVENTH HOUR," you:

a) put it off until the last minute.

b) do it at 11 a.m. or 11 p.m.

c) do your homework in study hall (eleventh hour is another name for study hall).

DOUBLE Z'S MARK THE SPOT

(5-15-72)

There are two Z's in the word PIZZA.

(HINT: You can choose your answers from the word box below.)

WORD BOX

PIZZA	PIZZAZZ	PUZZLE	QUIZZES
JAZZ	BUZZ	DAZZLE	DIZZY
FUZZY	BLIZZARD	FRIZZY	GRIZZLY
MUZZLE	FIZZY	MOZZARELLA	PIZZERIA

ACROSS

1. Snoopy's favorite food

2. a type of white cheese used to make pizza

3. a big and fierce type of bear

4. type of restaurant where you go to eat pizza

5. a really heavy snowstorm

6. _____ Wuzzy was a bear

7. what small tests are called

8. when a soda has a lot of bubbles, it's _____

DOWN

2. the snout of an animal (teeth, nose, jaw), or something you put over a dog's mouth so it won't bark or bite

4. the kind of activity you're doing right now

6. how your hair looks when it rains

9. very showy, with lots of flair (hint: this word is "pizza" plus two extra Z's)

10. to impress someone (hint: rhymes with razzle)

11. the noise a bee makes

12. music with a groovy beat

13. if you spin around in circles, you get _____

When Snoopy wears sunglasses and acts like a college student, he calls himself Joe Cool. Charles Schulz got the idea from his son, whose college classmates used the slang phrase "Joe Cool" whenever they were talking about someone popular and in control.

PIZZA TO THE RESCUE

Match each caption to the correct strip.

YOU WERE ROBBED!	I ALREADY ATE THE PIZZA...
SAVED BY A PIZZA!	WHAT'S THE NUMBER OF "VILLELLA'S TAKE-OUT PIZZA PARLOR"?

1.

(2-12-60)

2.

(2-13-60)

3.

(3-5-88)

4.

(3-14-88)

MATH MUNCHIES

What has Snoopy done to his doghouse?

Answer the questions below. Use the space to do your calculations, and write your answers in the boxes.

If each doghouse notch stands for 50 pizzas and there are four notches, how many pizzas did Snoopy eat?

$$50 \times 4 =$$

What if each of the four notches stands for 10 pizzas?

$$10 \times 4 =$$

Five pizzas?

$$5 \times 4 =$$

Twenty pizzas?

$$20 \times 4 =$$

LIGHTNING!

(9-24-84)

Pizza doesn't really attract lightning, but Snoopy is smart to go inside when the sky fills with lightning and thunder. Try this activity to understand what lightning is all about!

WHAT YOU DO:

1. Go inside a carpeted room. Turn off the lights and close the blinds if it is daylight outside.

2. Shuffle your feet across the carpet. You can wear shoes or just socks, but make sure you shuffle around a lot.

3. Touch a doorknob or some other metal object, like a key.

Did you see a spark?

That spark is like a little lightning bolt. Lightning is just a huge spark of electric current that happens when static electricity builds up in the air. This same static electricity builds up when you rub your feet on the carpet, or when the air changes from dry to wet (like in a rainstorm). Touching metal causes the spark because metal attracts electric charges (much better than pizza does, in fact!).

COMBINATION FUN

You already know how much Snoopy loves pizza. He loves doughnuts, too. But once in a while, even Snoopy likes to eat his favorite foods in a different order or combine them in new ways.

Practice your combining skills by drawing three lines in the box below to create four sections of numbers that each add up to 24.

2	5	5	9
8	9	2	5
5	8	9	2
2	9	8	8

HOMESICK FOR PIZZA

Snoopy can't live without pizza!

What can't you live without? Write or draw about it here:

SNOOPY'S PERFECT PARTY

(12-6-69)

Would you like to throw a party? Yours is sure to be a success if you follow these 10 tips (and don't invite snowmen!).

1. **START EARLY**
   Decide on a reason to have a party—like it's your birthday, the beginning of summer or winter, a holiday, or just because!

2. **PICK A THEME**
   Plan your party around something that sparks your interest or imagination. For example, you could have a Peanuts Party where everyone comes as their favorite Peanuts character. (Who would you be?)

3. **DECIDE ON A PLACE**
   How about a pizza parlor, farm, gym, nature center, or park?

4. **WRITE THE GUEST LIST**
   Sometimes you want to invite your whole class, but sometimes you just want to invite a few special friends.

5. **SEND INVITATIONS**
   Be sure to include the time, date, place, and reason for the party. Do you have the addresses of all your friends so they get your invitations in the mail?

6. **DECORATE**
   It's inexpensive and fun to make your own decorations out of colored paper or by using a lot of balloons. Be creative!

7. CHOOSE A MENU
   Keep things simple and stick with your theme.

8. BEGIN WITH A CRAFT PROJECT
   An activity will keep your guests busy until everyone arrives.

9. PLAN GAMES
   Alternate between quiet and active games
   (for example, first play a guessing game, then
   hold a relay race).

10. HAND OUT FAVORS AND PRIZES
    Simple gifts like penny candy and small toys are fine.

AND AFTER THE PARTY, IF YOU RECEIVED PRESENTS,
DON'T FORGET TO SEND THANK-YOU NOTES!!!

(8-29-82)

YOU'RE INVITED

When the invitation Snoopy receives says "regrets only," that means that he needs to let the person who invited him to the party know if he can't attend. Do you know how to send and receive an invitation? Here are some helpful hints:

 When you're planning a party, you should send your invitations a few weeks ahead of time. That way, your friends can make sure to be free on the day of the party.

 Your invitation should include the date, time, place, reason for the party, and anything else your guests might need to know, like if they need to bring a swimsuit or wear sneakers. The invitation should also include the letters R.S.V.P. That stands for Répondez s'il vous plaît, which is French for "please respond" ("reply, if it pleases you," to be exact!). Unless the invitation says "regrets only," like Snoopy's does, you should always let the person who invited you know if you are—or are not—going to attend the party.

 Homemade invitations are fun to make. Draw an invitation for the next party you'd like to have.

YOU'RE INVITED
TO A PIZZA PARTY!

DATE: March 3, 2003

TIME: 12 p.m. - 2 p.m.

PLACE: Snoopy's House

PLEASE R.S.V.P. BY FEB. 2
222-555-1234

FORGET THE PARTY

Violet is having a party. Everyone is invited—except for Charlie Brown.

Violet, one of Charlie Brown's classmates, was one of the first characters Charles Schulz created. Poor Charlie Brown. Violet certainly makes his life difficult! Maybe when Charlie Brown sits at home while everyone else is at Violet's party, he can have fun with this crossword puzzle based on party words.

(**HINT:** You can choose your answers from the word box below.)

WORD BOX

PIZZA	CRAFT	FRIENDS
SLUMBER	FOOD	PRESENT
MUSIC	GAME	CAKE
FAVOR	INVITATION	ICE CREAM
PIÑATA		

ACROSS

1. what Snoopy sometimes eats at midnight

2. you put candles on this party food

3. who you invite to your party

4. you send this in the mail to announce your party

5. an art project

6. something you play at a party

7. a yummy frozen dessert (two words)

DOWN

1. another word for gift

3. what no party should be without when you get hungry

8. if you break this Mexican party game, you won't get in trouble (hint: you're supposed to break it open to get to the prizes inside)

9. another name for a sleepover is a _____ party

10. you can't dance without it

11. a take-home present for your guests is a party _____

SURPRISE!

What is Snoopy getting into?

(8-10-68)

The Peanuts Gang planned a surprise party for Snoopy. What do you think Snoopy thought in the last caption of the strip? To find out, first do the math problems and write the answers in the boxes below. Then use the code to find the letter that corresponds to each number. Write the letters in the spaces to find out what Snoopy thought.

CODE:

1 = E	4 = S	7 = B	10 = W	13 = O
2 = I	5 = R	8 = A	11 = G	14 = L
3 = P	6 = U	9 = Y	12 = D	15 = N

___ ___ ___ ___ , ___ ' ___ ___ ___ ___ ___

5+5	8-7	7+7	10+4	5-3	9+5	20-6	6+1	9-8	4+4
☐	☐	☐	☐	☐	☐	☐	☐	☐	☐

___ ___ ___ ___ ___ — ___ ___ ___ ___

10-3	7-2	6+7	19-9	7+8		2-1	4+5	1+0	6+6
☐	☐	☐	☐	☐		☐	☐	☐	☐

___ ___ ___ ___ ___ ___ !

4+3	7-6	5+3	7+4	8+6	13-12
☐	☐	☐	☐	☐	☐

WATCH OUT—HERE COMES PIGPEN!

(6-17-62)

What's the perfect treat to serve Pigpen at a party?
Looks like he'd love a mud pie! You can make this yummy recipe.

MUD PIE

(makes 8-10 servings)

WHAT YOU NEED:

1 quart chocolate ice cream

1 cup whipped cream topping

ready-made chocolate cookie
  pie crust

3 or 4 chocolate cookies,
  crushed

½ cup fudge topping

gummy worms (optional)

You'll also need a spatula and measuring cups.

WHAT YOU DO:

1. Remove the ice cream from the freezer and let it soften for 10 minutes.

2. Spread the softened ice cream into the pie crust with the spatula.

3. Spread the fudge topping across the ice cream.

4. Spread the whipped cream topping across the fudge.

5. Sprinkle the crushed cookies across the whipped cream.

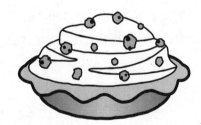

6. Put the mud pie in the freezer for at least an hour.

7. Slice and serve!

For a surprise treat, hide some gummy worms in the ice cream!

EVERYONE IN THE POOL!!

(7-28-75)

Snoopy may hate swim parties, but if you play these games at your next pool party, it's sure to be a splash!

Before you begin, make sure that everyone who wants to play knows how to swim, and that a lifeguard or another adult is around to watch (and act as a referee).

CUBE COUNT

WHAT YOU NEED:

2 plastic bowls

2 doughnut-shaped inflatable pool floats (so that a bowl will fit in the middle)

a timer

1 large bag of ice cubes

4-10 players

WHAT YOU DO:

Divide the players into two teams and have each team line up on an opposite side of the pool. For each team, place a plastic bowl inside a pool float. Have an adult referee set the timer for three minutes, and dump the large bag of ice cubes into the pool. When the referee says "go," players rush to collect ice cubes and carry them to their team's bowl in the pool float. The team that collects the most ice cubes in its bowl at the end of three minutes is the winner.

Be careful not to run into other players!

TREASURE HUNT

WHAT YOU NEED:

little objects that sink
(coins, keys, spoons)
and some that float
(sponge balls)

a timer

4-10 players

WHAT YOU DO:

Divide the players into two teams. Give each team a list
of objects. Set the timer for five minutes, then throw
the objects into the pool (some in the deep end for
strong swimmers, some in the shallow end for beginners).
The team that collects the most objects on their list by
the end of five minutes wins.

PING

WHAT YOU NEED:

a permanent/waterproof
  marker

20 ping-pong balls

2 buckets or bowls

4-10 players

WHAT YOU DO:

With the permanent marker, write the numbers 1 through 5 on
the 20 ping-pong balls (write the number 1 on four balls, the
number 2 on four balls, and so on). Divide the players into two
teams. Each team lines up along opposite sides of the pool. Dump
the balls in the middle of the pool. Teams hurry to collect the
ping-pong balls and carry them to the bucket or bowl on their
side of the pool. (Important: players can only carry one ball at a
time.) When all the balls have been collected, add up the numbers
written on the balls. The team with the highest score wins.

BREAKFAST BASH

(2-26-61)

Here's a new party idea. After a good night's sleep, have your friends come over for some breakfast fun!

- Invite your friends to come over early in the morning, dressed in their pajamas.

- Serve pancakes or waffles.

- Have a pillow fight or decorate pillowcases with fabric markers.

- Watch some morning cartoons or your favorite videos.

- For an extra treat, make the breakfast sundaes on the next page!

BREAKFAST SUNDAES

(5-15-71)

WHAT YOU NEED: (for each sundae)

plain or vanilla yogurt
  (½ cup for each sundae)

fresh fruit (berries, bananas,
  peaches, apples, melon)

granola

mini marshmallows
  or marshmallow fluff

maraschino cherry

You'll also need a parfait glass
(that's a fancy glass like the one shown, but any clear drinking glass will do!).

WHAT YOU DO:

1. For each sundae, put ¼ cup of yogurt at the bottom of a parfait glass.

2. Put cut fresh fruit on top of the yogurt.

3. Put another ¼ cup of yogurt on top of the fruit.

4. Sprinkle with granola.

5. Decorate with mini marshmallows or a dab of marshmallow fluff.

6. Top with a cherry.

7. Enjoy!

FLAT AS A PANCAKE

FLIP-FLOP

(5-15-93)

Snoopy always knows how to show his troops a good time on their camping trips. Try this relay race at your next outdoor outing, picnic, or party!

PANCAKE RELAY

WHAT YOU NEED:

2 pancakes   4-10 players
  (or 2 pieces of cardboard,
  cut into large circles)

2 metal or plastic spatulas

WHAT YOU DO:

1. Divide the players into two teams.

2. Select a starting line and a turnaround line.

3. Line up behind the starting line.

4. The first player on each team holds a pancake on a spatula and walks (or runs carefully) to the turnaround line and back. If the player drops the pancake, he must start over at the starting line.

5. The first player hands off the spatula and pancake to the next person in line. The second person must do the same thing.

6. The first team to have all its players cross the finish line (which is the same as the starting line) with the pancake wins!

WHAT'S FOR LUNCH?

Panel 1: ...AND AN APPLE AND SOME CARROTS..

Panel 2: WHAT DO YOU HAVE?

Panel 3: A TUNA FLAT SANDWICH.. © 1987 United Feature Syndicate, Inc. 10-19

Panel 4: THE SCHOOL BUS RAN OVER MY LUNCH BOX!

(10-19-87)

Sally didn't make a Tuna Flat Sandwich on purpose, but you can!

SALLY'S TUNA FLAT SANDWICH

(makes 1 sandwich)

WHAT YOU NEED:

1 can tuna packed in water (drained)

2 tablespoons mayonnaise

$\frac{1}{2}$ onion, chopped (optional)

$\frac{1}{4}$ teaspoon lemon juice

2 slices bread

You'll also need a bowl, measuring spoons, a fork, a knife, a rolling pin, and a plastic bag (optional).

WHAT YOU DO:

1. In the bowl, combine the tuna, mayonnaise, onion, and lemon juice with the fork.

2. Cut the crusts off the bread and flatten each slice with the rolling pin.

3. Spread a thin layer of the tuna mixture on one slice of bread.

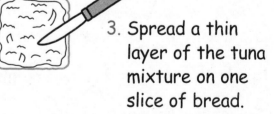

4. Top with the other slice of bread to complete your flat sandwich.

5. Eat your sandwich right away, or seal it in a plastic bag for your lunch box lunch.

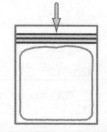

PANCAKES FOR LUNCH? WELL, MAYBE.

(10-20-87)

YUMMY BUTTERMILK PANCAKES

(makes two dozen 3-inch pancakes)

WHAT YOU NEED:

2 cups buttermilk

2 eggs

1 tablespoon oil
   or melted butter

1¼ cups flour

1½ teaspoon baking powder

1 teaspoon baking soda

1 teaspoon sugar

¼ teaspoon salt

butter to grease the pan

You'll also need a medium bowl, measuring cups and spoons, a spoon, a whisk, a ladle, a frying pan (or griddle), a spatula, foil (optional) and an adult to help.

WHAT YOU DO:

1. In the medium bowl, stir together the buttermilk, eggs, and oil or butter with a spoon.

2. Add the flour, baking powder, baking soda, sugar, and salt to the wet ingredients in the bowl.

3. Stir all of the ingredients with the whisk.

4. Preheat and butter a frying pan (or griddle) on medium heat.

5. Ladle the mixture into the frying pan in big or little scoops.

6. When the top of each scoop begins to bubble, flip the pancake with the spatula and cook the other side until it's golden brown.

7. Serve your pancakes immediately, or wrap in foil and bring to school for lunch!

NOTE: If you don't have buttermilk, add one teaspoon lemon juice to regular milk.

LUNCH BELL

How would *you* carry your sandwich to school if your lunch box was broken and you had no more brown paper bags? Come up with your own clever ideas. Write or draw them here.

_____

_____

_____

_____

FIELD TRIP

(1-23-84)

In this strip, Charles Schulz drew Sally and her classmate in profile. Your *profile* is a side view of your face. Here is a great way to draw a profile:

WHAT YOU NEED:

tape	a flashlight	a marker
piece of paper	a pencil	

WHAT YOU DO:

1. Ask a friend or family member to sit in a chair facing sideways about three feet away from a blank wall.

2. Tape a large piece of paper to the wall at about the same height as your seated friend's head.

3. Position a flashlight on a table so that its light shines in the direction of your subject and the shadow of the profile appears on the piece of paper. (This is called a *silhouette*.) You can also turn on a lamp to cast your friend's shadow on the wall.

4. Use the pencil to trace around the silhouette on the paper.

5. Take the paper down from the wall and go over the pencil line with a marker.

6. You can leave the silhouette as it is, shade it in, or add details like an eye, lips, an ear, and hair if you want. Remember, as an artist, you make all the decisions!

7. Once you've traced a couple of shadow profiles, see if you can draw these profiles of the Peanuts Gang!

HOT BREAKFAST

Snoopy likes breakfast time almost as much as he likes suppertime!

Cold cereal just doesn't satisfy Snoopy on a snowy morning!
Use the clues to fill in this crossword puzzle with hot breakfast foods.
If you need help, check out the word box.

(HINT: You can choose your answers from the word box below.)

WORD BOX

TOAST	OMELETTE
WAFFLE	MUFFIN
OATMEAL	HOT CHOCOLATE
EGGS	GRITS
PANCAKE	BACON

ACROSS

1. a kind of hot cereal

2. small cake-like breakfast bread

3. a warm drink (two words)

4. these can be sunny side up, scrambled, or hard boiled

5. grilled bread

DOWN

6. Southern corn cereal

7. another word for flapjack

8. eggs cooked in a pan, folded over and often with a filling

9. breakfast food with little squares that you pour syrup in

10. crispy and salty breakfast meat

CEREAL BOX CITY

Eating breakfast is hard work!

You can be creative with your cereal box, too. You can make a model of Snoopy's house, Ace Elementary School, or any other buildings you've seen in Charles Schulz's strips.

WHAT YOU NEED:

empty cereal boxes

paper (brown paper bags,
  construction paper,
  wrapping paper, etc.)

tape

crayons or markers

a large sheet of paper
  or poster board

WHAT YOU DO:

1. Wrap the empty cereal boxes in paper.

2. Tape the paper in place.

3. Draw windows, doors, and other details.

4. Arrange the "buildings" on a large sheet of paper or poster board.

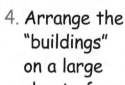

5. Draw streets, lawns, and road signs on the sheet of paper to surround your buildings.

TIP: Milk cartons covered in paper make great houses, too. See what else you can find in the kitchen to use!

PICTURE CHARADES

(12-28-90)

Snoopy does a fine imitation of toast popping out of a toaster!
When you play this game, you can act like Snoopy.

WHAT YOU NEED:

old magazines   15-20 index cards

scissors   2 or more players

glue stick

WHAT YOU DO:

1. Before you play, look through old magazines and cut out pictures of objects and animals.

2. Glue the pictures to index cards.

3. Place the cards in a deck, picture-side down. Shuffle the deck.

4. The first player picks a card, being careful not to let any of the other players see it.

5. The player must silently act out whatever picture is on the card.

6. Whoever correctly guesses what the player is acting out becomes the next person to act out a picture.

How would you act out a car? A television? An elephant? A pizza?

INTO THE FRYING PAN

(10-7-54)

If Lucy knew this recipe, she might enjoy eating her whole piece of bread!

EGGS IN A NEST

(makes 1 serving)

WHAT YOU NEED:

1 slice bread	1 egg
1 teaspoon butter	salt and pepper to taste

You'll also need a cookie cutter, frying pan,
spatula, and an adult to help you.

WHAT YOU DO:

1. Use the cookie cutter to cut a shape out of the center of the bread. Then set the cut-out shape aside.

2. Melt the butter in the frying pan over medium heat.

3. Place the bread with the hole in it in the pan and crack the egg into the hole.

4. Sprinkle the egg with salt and pepper.

5. When the egg is cooked on one side, flip it over with the spatula to cook the other side (about a minute each side).

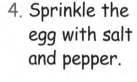

TIP: You can toast the cut-out shape in the pan, too!

SNOOPY'S CHOICE

Watch out, Snoopy—here comes Charlie Brown.

(1-4-81)

What might Snoopy rather eat for breakfast than a pancake on his nose?
Follow the instructions below to find out.

CIRCLE:

- The first letter of every item you might find on the kitchen table.
- The second letter of every color.
- The third letter of every body part.
- The fourth letter of every animal or insect.

YELLOW	HAND	GLASS
BLUE	PINK	MOOSE
MOTH	ARM	PURPLE
BUFFALO	FORK	CHIN
NAPKIN		

Now write the circled letters in order, line by line, from left to right beginning with the upper lefthand box, below.

Snoopy could eat an _____ _____ .

MARCIE YOLKS IT UP

Peppermint Patty often falls asleep in class.
Marcie has some advice for Peppermint Patty.

(3-3-78)

Marcie may have to work on her joke-telling skills a bit.
Here are some more chicken and egg jokes she can try next time.

WHY DID THE CHICKEN
CROSS THE ROAD?

Because the rooster egged her on.

WHY DID THE TURKEY
CROSS THE ROAD?

To prove he wasn't chicken.

WHY DID THE HORSE
CROSS THE ROAD?

The chicken needed a day off.

WHY DID THE CHICKEN
CROSS THE PLAYGROUND?

To get to the other slide.

IF A ROOSTER LAID AN EGG ON
THE TOP OF A BARN, WHICH WAY
WOULD IT ROLL?

It wouldn't. Roosters don't lay eggs!

WHERE DID THE CHICKEN GO
ON VACATION?

Sandy-Eggo.

WHAT DO YOU CALL AN EGG
THAT GOES ON A SAFARI?

An eggs-plorer.

WHAT HAPPENS WHEN YOU
TELL AN EGG A JOKE?

It cracks up.

Add your own favorite chicken
and egg jokes here:

_____

_____

_____

_____

PRESTO CHANGO

It's always handy to have a dog around—at least a dog like Snoopy!

Even if the strip didn't include Snoopy's thought bubbles, you'd still know the toast was hot because of the action lines Charles Schulz drew to show what happens in each picture when Snoopy touches the bread.

Practice your own cartooning skills on the next page.

Add details to this picture.

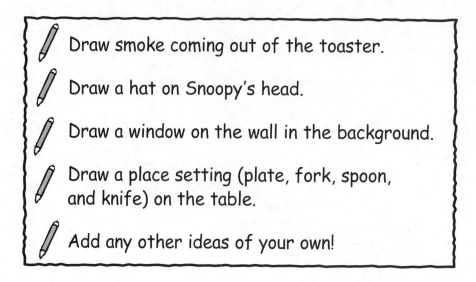

✏️ Draw smoke coming out of the toaster.

✏️ Draw a hat on Snoopy's head.

✏️ Draw a window on the wall in the background.

✏️ Draw a place setting (plate, fork, spoon, and knife) on the table.

✏️ Add any other ideas of your own!

WAFFLE WORLD

(10-13-98) Rerun wouldn't be a starving artist if he created art with waffles!

WAFFLE ART

WHAT YOU NEED:

2 frozen square
or rectangular waffles

2 – 4 tablespoons
peanut butter and jelly

You'll also need a toaster, a table knife,
and waxed paper (or a large plate).

WHAT YOU DO:

1. Toast the waffles and let them cool.

2. Using the squares in the waffles as a guide, cut the waffles into different sized pieces.

3. Place the pieces next to each other on the waxed paper (or a large plate) and connect them with peanut butter "glue" to create houses and other buildings.

4. Highlight windows and doors using jelly.

5. Eat your creation!

51

PEANUT BUTTER PLAY DOUGH

Next time you feel nervous, you can fiddle with edible peanut butter play dough.

WHAT YOU NEED: (makes 1½ cups)

1 cup creamy peanut butter   3 tablespoons honey

1½ cups powdered milk

You'll also need a medium bowl, a wooden spoon, measuring cups and spoons, an airtight container, and clean hands (so wash them before you start!).

WHAT YOU DO:

1. In the medium bowl, mix all the ingredients together with the wooden spoon.

3. Roll small pieces of the dough into any shapes you want.

4. When you're done playing, you can eat your masterpieces!

2. Continue stirring until the mixture resembles the consistency of play dough. (If it's too dry, add more honey. If it's too sticky, add more powdered milk.)

5. Store whatever you don't eat in an airtight container in the refrigerator.

Charlie Brown always gets nervous at the sight of the little girl with red hair because he has a huge crush on her, but her face never actually appears in the PEANUTS strips. Charles Schulz's inspiration for the little red haired girl came from a red haired woman he dated when he was young.

A PEANUT BUTTER WHAT?

(5-8-75)

A peanut butter doughnut doesn't sound too good.
But how about Peanut Butter Crispy Rice Bars?

PEANUT BUTTER CRISPY RICE BARS

(makes 36 squares)

WHAT YOU NEED:

butter to grease the pan

¼ cup butter

1 package (10 oz.) marshmallows

6 cups crispy puffed rice cereal

1 bag (10 oz.) peanutbutter chips

½ cup chopped peanuts

You'll also need a 13 x 9 inch baking pan, measuring cups, a large pot, a wooden mixing spoon, and an adult to help you.

WHAT YOU DO:

1. Grease the baking pan.

2. Melt the butter in the large pot over low heat. Add the marshmallows. Stir until melted.

3. Remove from the heat and stir in the cereal, peanut butter chips, and peanuts. Mix well.

4. Pour the mixture into the pan and use the spoon to press it out to the edges.

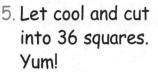

5. Let cool and cut into 36 squares. Yum!

PICNIC ANTS

(6-2-58)

Maybe Snoopy needs to eat some ants so he can have their energy. You can eat ants, too! In this recipe, raisins will be the "ants."

ANTS ON A LOG

(make as many logs as you like)

> ### WHAT YOU NEED:
> celery sticks   raisins
> peanut butter

You'll also need a knife, and an adult to help you slice.

WHAT YOU DO:

1. Wash the celery and cut it into pieces about five inches long.

2. Spread peanut butter on the celery.

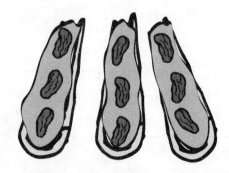

3. Press raisins (ants) into the peanut butter. Enjoy!

54

PEANUT BUTTER AND ADVICE

Linus's mom is at it again!

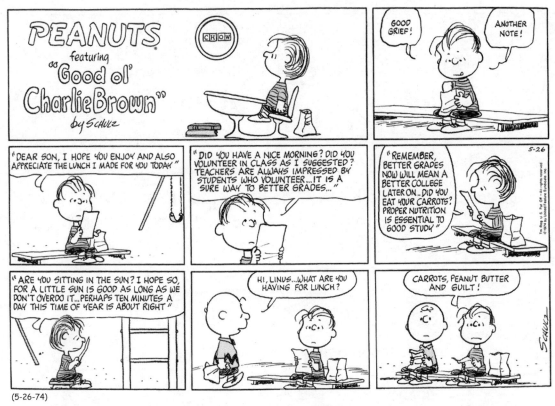

Poor Linus! His mom is constantly filling his lunch bag with advice. Have you ever received a note in your lunch?

Or, have you ever tried carrots with peanut butter? How do you think it would taste? Write or draw your thoughts here:

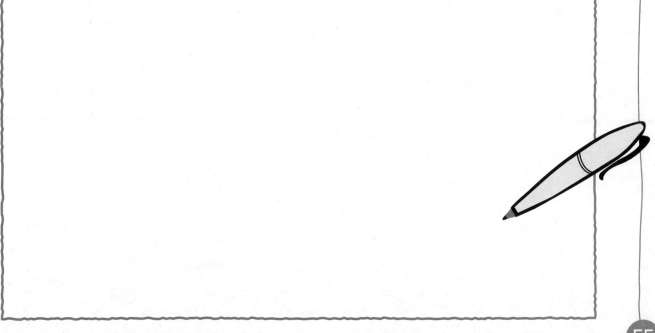

PEANUT BUTTER TWIST

Same old, same old.

(2-17-81)

If you can't stand the thought of just another plain old peanut butter sandwich, try one of these peanut butter variations:

PEANUT BUTTER AND...

1 tablespoon honey

$\frac{1}{2}$ a banana, peeled and sliced

1 teaspoon chocolate chips

$\frac{1}{2}$ an apple, cored and thinly sliced

1 tablespoon marshmallow fluff

$\frac{1}{2}$ a carrot, peeled and grated

1 tablespoon flaked coconut

crushed potato chips (really, it tastes great!)

1 tablespoon apple butter

HERE'S ANOTHER IDEA:

Instead of your regular peanut butter, try cashew butter, almond butter, or hazelnut butter instead!

ARACHIBUTYROPHOBIA?!?!

Match each caption to the correct strip.
Then, learn more about this mouthful of a word!

> WHEN YOU'RE REAL LONELY, THE PEANUT BUTTER STICKS TO THE ROOF OF YOUR MOUTH...

> THIS IS THE FEAR OF PEANUT BUTTER STICKING TO THE ROOF OF YOUR MOUTH, AND MAY BE A BEAUTIFUL EXCUSE FOR NOT GOING TO SCHOOL SOME DAY...

1.

(11-11-63)

2.

(5-19-82)

Arachibutyrophobia is—*no joke!*—the fear of peanut butter sticking to the roof of your mouth. A phobia is a fear of something that causes people to avoid it. Does peanut butter stick to the roof of *your* mouth when you eat it? Does drinking milk help wash the peanut butter down?

(2-3-58)

PEANUT BUTTER PASS

Snoopy will do *anything* to snatch a good peanut butter cookie.

THE BEST PEANUT BUTTER COOKIES EVER

(makes 3-4 dozen)

WHAT YOU NEED:

butter to grease the
  cookie sheets

2 cups creamy peanut butter

2 cups sugar

2 eggs

2 teaspoons baking soda

pinch of salt

1 teaspoon vanilla

You'll also need two cookie sheets, measuring cups and spoons, a medium bowl,
an electric mixer (or lots of energy to mix with your hands), a small bowl,
a fork, a big spoon, a ruler, and an adult to help you.

WHAT YOU DO:

1. Preheat the oven to 350°F and grease two cookie sheets.

2. Put the peanut butter and sugar in the medium bowl and beat with an electric mixer until fluffy. (If you don't have a mixer, ask an adult to help you stir the peanut butter and sugar with a big spoon.)

3. Crack the eggs into the small bowl and stir them rapidly with a fork, until the yolks and whites are blended.

4. Beat the eggs into the butter and sugar mixture, and then beat in the baking soda, salt, and vanilla.

5. Roll the dough into balls about one inch in diameter and place them two inches apart on the cookie sheets. With the tines (the prongs) of the fork, press lines into the balls to flatten them.

6. Bake for 10 minutes or until the cookies are puffy and golden brown. Yum!

MARSHMALLOW RELAY

(7-19-73)

Looks like Snoopy could use a little picnic help.
But at least Woodstock knows the importance of marshmallows!
Here's a fun activity to do with those chewy, gooey, white things:

WHAT YOU NEED:

a spoon for each player

2 or more players

10 marshmallows
for each player

WHAT YOU DO:

1. Mark off a starting line and finish line in an open space, like your family room, basement, front yard, or driveway.

2. Have the players line up at the starting line.

3. Each player must carry 10 marshmallows on a spoon across the finish line. You can carry them one at a time or stack them. If you drop any, you have to start all over again.

4. The first player to carry all 10 marshmallows across the finish line without dropping any is the winner!

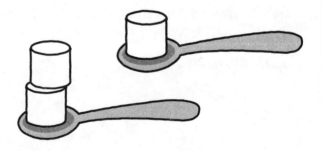

READY, SET, GO!

MARSHMALLOW MAKEOVER

(5-26-80)

If Peppermint Patty gets tired of eating the marshmallows in her lunch, she can always play with her food!

MARSHMALLOW SNOWPERSON

WHAT YOU NEED:

large marshmallows	gumdrops
thin stick pretzels	fruit leather
candy bits	licorice sticks

WHAT YOU DO:

1. Stack three marshmallows and push a pretzel stick through the center of the stack to start your snowperson.

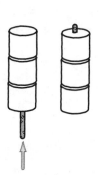

2. Stick two more pretzel pieces into the sides of the middle marshmallow for arms.

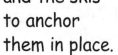

3. Press on candy bits for facial features and buttons.

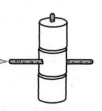

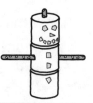

4. Make a hat out of gumdrops and cut a scarf out of fruit leather.

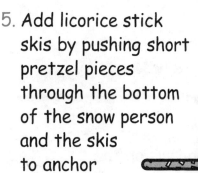

5. Add licorice stick skis by pushing short pretzel pieces through the bottom of the snow person and the skis to anchor them in place.

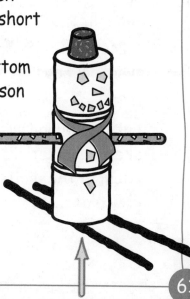

MARSHMALLOWS ON A STICK

(12-26-89)

Sally can get a double dose of chocolate
on her marshmallows with this recipe.

CHOCOLATE MARSHMALLOWS
(serves 10)

WHAT YOU NEED:

one 10 oz. package of semisweet
  chocolate chips

large marshmallows

hot chocolate (optional)

You'll also need a saucepan, skewers or sticks, and an adult to help you.

WHAT YOU DO:

1. Melt the chocolate chips in the saucepan over low heat.

2. Put marshmallows on the skewers or sticks and dip them in the melted chocolate.

3. Let the marshmallows cool a few moments before you eat them.

4. You can get a double dose of chocolate by double-dipping your chocolate-covered marshmallows in your hot chocolate, if you like!

A BUNCH OF MARSHMALLOWS

..AND WHILE WE'RE SETTING UP CAMP, CONRAD WILL START TO ROAST THE MARSHMALLOWS...

BUT IT WOULD BE BETTER IF HE JUST ROASTED THEM ONE AT A TIME..

© 1990 United Feature Syndicate, Inc.

4-5

(4-5-90)

That isn't just *any* bunch of marshmallows—it's a Marshmallow Popcorn Ball!

MARSHMALLOW POPCORN BALL

WHAT YOU NEED: (makes 8-10 balls)

5 cups popcorn, popped

½ cup mini chocolate chips or M&M's

½ cup peanuts

2 tablespoons butter or margarine, softened

3 cups marshmallows

You'll also need measuring cups and spoons, a large bowl, a saucepan, a spoon, waxed paper, clean hands, and an adult to help.

WHAT YOU DO:

1. Combine the popcorn, chocolate chips or M&M's, and peanuts in the large bowl.

2. Place the butter and marshmallows in the saucepan or a 4-cup microwave-safe measuring cup.

3. Heat over low heat until melted and smooth (stir at least once halfway through cooking), or microwave on high for two minutes.

4. Pour the butter-marshmallow mixture over the popcorn mixture; stir quickly to coat.

5. With clean, buttered hands, shape the mixture into 8-10 balls. Place on waxed paper. Let cool.

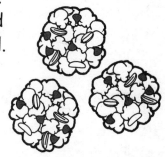

MARSHMALLOW MANIA!

Marcie is prepared to survive in the wilderness.

Marcie's bag is stuffed with marshmallows so she can make lots of yummy s'mores while camping! You can make s'mores in the woods or at home.

S'MORES

WHAT YOU NEED: (for each s'more)

1 marshmallow   2 graham cracker squares

½ milk chocolate bar

You'll also need a campfire and a stick, or an oven
and a cookie sheet, and an adult to help you.

WHAT YOU DO:

1. Toast the marshmallow over the coals of a campfire (or put it in the oven on a cookie sheet at 250°F for two minutes) until golden brown.

2. Put the toasted marshmallow on the chocolate bar and sandwich them between the two graham cracker squares.

3. Enjoy! Be prepared to lick your fingers when you're done!

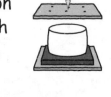

S'MORE VARIATIONS:

- Spread peanut butter on the graham crackers (with or without the chocolate).

- Use chocolate-covered graham crackers.

- Use chocolate-covered mints instead of a chocolate bar.

- Add banana slices.

- Instead of toasting the marshmallows in the oven, microwave them on high for 10-15 seconds on a microwave-safe plate.

THE JOY OF EATING

PEANUTS

I'VE HEARD THE REPORTS...

I'VE READ ALL THE ARTICLES...

I DON'T CARE WHAT ANYONE SAYS...

ONE OF THE GREAT JOYS IN LIFE IS SCARFING

(5-26-75)

What is a joy for Snoopy to eat? To find out, first use the clues to fill in the puzzle answers and add them to the puzzle grid. Then write all of the letters in the puzzle grid circles in the spaces below.
(HINT: The answer is two words.)

1. another word for jelly

2. opposite of down

3. if it's not the beginning, it's the _____

4. a windy day is the best time to fly a _____

5. opposite of on

6. a large musical instrument with black and white keys

7. opposite of close (as in "close the door")

8. when you are thirsty, it helps to take a _____ of water

ANSWER: ☐ ☐ ☐ ☐ ☐ ☐ ☐ ☐

CRAZY COMBINATIONS

Make up your own crazy food combinations.
What can you make with spaghetti as the main ingredient?
How about ice cream? Write your ideas here.

SPAGHETTI COMBOS

_____

_____

_____

_____

_____

ICE CREAM COMBOS

_____

_____

_____

_____

_____

ADD YOUR OWN COMBOS HERE:

_____

_____

_____

_____

_____

_____

DRAW YOUR OWN DOUGHNUT

(1-25-82)

This picture of Snoopy is all mixed up. Use the blank grid to put Snoopy and his doughnut back together! Pick a square on the scrambled grid. Find the same numbered square on the empty grid and copy exactly what you see into the blank space. Repeat for each square until you have completed the picture!

1.	2.	3.
4.	5.	6.
7.	8.	9.

LOST LUNCH

YES, MA'AM, I LEFT MY LUNCH BOX ON THE CURB BY THE BUS STOP...

1-23

(1-23-86)

SOMEONE'S PROBABLY FOUND IT BY NOW

I JUST HOPE WHOEVER FOUND IT APPRECIATES A GOOD LUNCH...

© 1986 United Feature Syndicate, Inc.

NO _____ !?!

What was Snoopy hoping to find in Sally's lunch box? See if you can find out by breaking this code, which is called Morse code. Write the letter that matches each symbol in the spaces below to find out the correct answer. A slash (/) is used after each letter in the word. What word is it?

A	.−	J	.−−−	S	...
B	−...	K	−.−	T	−
C	−.−.	L	.−−.	U	..−
D	−..	M	−−	V	...−
E	.	N	−.	W	.−−
F	..−.	O	−−−	X	−..−
G	−−.	P	.−−.	Y	−.−−
H	....	Q	−−.−	Z	−−..
I	..	R	.−.		

−../ −−−/ ..−/ −−./ ..../ −./ ..−/ −/ ...

___ ___ ___ ___ ___ ___ ___ ___ ___

POP, POP, POPCORN

(12-27-77)

Meet Schroeder. He's an amazing classical piano player. Lucy has a huge crush on him, but Schroeder's not interested in anything but his toy piano. Perhaps Schroeder would say yes to Lucy's invitation if she made Nacho Popcorn. Yum!

NACHO POPCORN

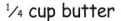

WHAT YOU NEED:

¼ cup butter

½ teaspoon paprika

½ teaspoon cumin

⅛ teaspoon red pepper flakes

10 cups popcorn, popped

½ cup Parmesan cheese

You'll also need measuring cups and spoons, a saucepan (or a microwave safe bowl), a spoon, a large bowl, an airtight container, and an adult to help you.

WHAT YOU DO:

1. Melt the butter over medium heat in the saucepan, or place it in a microwave-safe bowl and heat it on high for 30 seconds.

2. Add the paprika, cumin, and red pepper flakes to the melted butter and stir until blended.

3. Toss the popcorn in the large bowl with the spicy butter mix and the Parmesan cheese.

4. Store whatever popcorn you don't eat in an airtight container.

CHARLES M. SCHULZ ON SCHROEDER:

"Schroeder, who idolizes Beethoven, brought classical music to the Peanuts strip....

"Schroeder just seemed right for the character in the strip even before he became the great musician he is now. The idea came from a toy piano I gave my daughter Meredith."

SEED SPIT

(7-21-93)

Here is a fun and silly game to play the next time you are sharing a watermelon with a crowd.

WHAT YOU NEED:

a marker

a watermelon

a bottle cap for each player

2 or more players

Before you play, write each player's initials on the top of a bottle cap.

One at a time, players stand at a starting line and spit one watermelon seed as far as possible. Place each player's bottle cap over the seed they spat, to mark the spot. The player who spits the farthest wins! Celebrate by eating your (now seedless) watermelon!

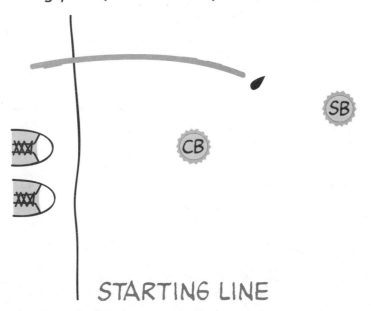

STARTING LINE

FRUIT FUN

Peppermint Patty and Marcie are having fruity fun in school—
maybe a little *too* much fun!

Here's another way to have fun with fruit.

FUN FRUIT KABOBS
(makes 10 kabobs)

WHAT YOU NEED:

2 bananas

2 apples

½ pineapple

10 strawberries

green and red grapes

vanilla or fruit flavored
  yogurt

shredded coconut

You'll also need a knife to slice the fruit, wooden skewers,
two plates, and an adult to help you.

WHAT YOU DO:

1. Wash the fruit. Peel and slice the bananas. Cut the apples and pineapple into chunks. Cut the strawberries in half. Pick grapes off the bunch.

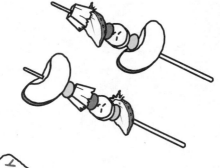

2. Slide pieces of fruit onto the skewers. Have fun making patterns!

3. Pour the yogurt onto one plate and spread the coconut onto the second plate.

4. Hold the ends of each fruit kabob skewer and roll it first into the yogurt, then into the coconut.

TASTY!

Do you know what the real expression—comparing apples and oranges—means? Although apples and oranges are both fruits, they are not alike in terms of their color, taste, or texture. So when someone says something is like comparing apples and oranges, it means that two things are so different that it's hard to find any similarities between them.

FRUIT SALAD MIX-UP

Peppermint Patty is having teacher trouble again.

Use the picture clues to fill in this fruity crossword puzzle.

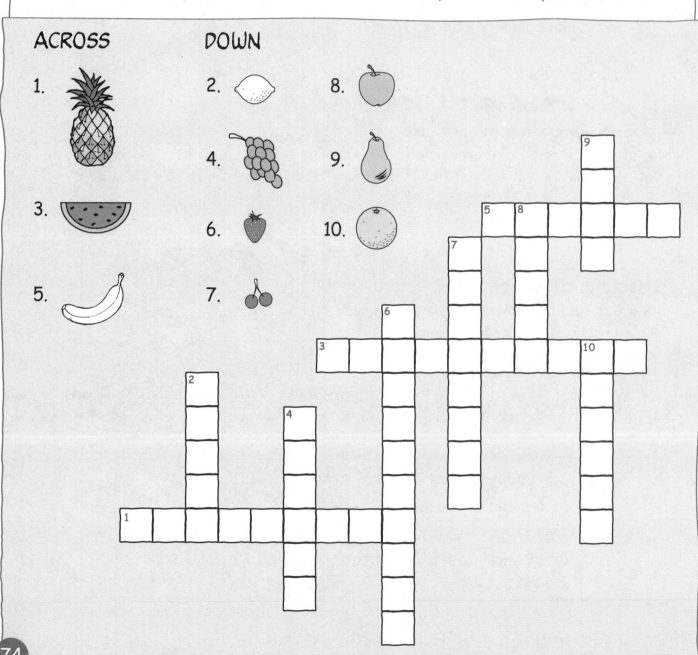

ACROSS

1.

3.

5.

DOWN

2.

4.

6.

7.

8.

9.

10.

BANANA BUNCH

Charlie Brown to the rescue!

(9-7-73)

Follow the maze through the banana bunch from start to finish.

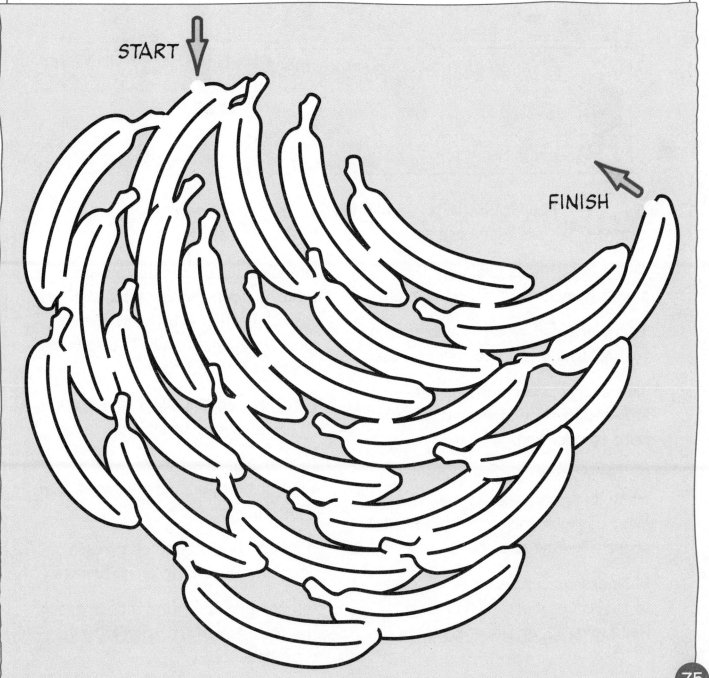

START

FINISH

BANANA BOOMERANG

YOU'RE VERY WEIRD, SIR... BUT AMUSING...

(10-4-92)

Peppermint Patty thinks her banana is a boomerang.
Here are some facts about boomerangs:

- The boomerang is probably the oldest human-made flying machine.

- There are two types of boomerangs: the returning and the nonreturning.

- Nonreturning boomerangs are long and heavy and were originally used for hunting.

- Returning boomerangs come in many different shapes, but the most common shape is the banana shape, like the one above.

- Boomerangs can be made of lots of different materials, like light wood, plastic, or fiberglass.

- There's a lot of physics involved in how a boomerang works, but basically, when you throw one, it spins through the air. The spinning makes it lift and turn.

- Throwing a boomerang isn't easy. It takes lots of practice.

- Boomerangs are thrown with the same basic overhand throw used in other sports.

- It's best to practice on a warm, clear day with little or no breeze.

- You can probably find a boomerang at a local toy store—don't try to use a banana!

76

CATCH THIS

Well, it *looked* just like a baseball...

(8-9-64)

Maybe Linus would have better luck at jump rope than at baseball.
Here is a jump rope rhyme about this cartoon strip.
Now you choose a strip and make up a rhyme about it.

AS I CLIMBED UP THE APPLE TREE,

ALL THE APPLES FELL ON ME.

BEFORE ONE APPLE HIT THE GROUND,

I THREW IT BACK TO CHARLIE BROWN.

CARROT CAKE

(5-13-88)

Carrot muffins aren't vegetables either, but they sure taste good!

CARROT MUFFINS

WHAT YOU NEED: (makes 18 muffins)

3 cups flour

2 teaspoons baking powder

½ teaspoon baking soda

½ teaspoon salt

½ teaspoon cinnamon

½ teaspoon nutmeg

2 cups white sugar

1¼ cups vegetable oil

4 eggs, lightly beaten

2 cups grated carrots

½ cup raisins

You'll also need a large bowl, measuring cups and spoons, a mixing spoon, muffin tins, and an adult to help.

WHAT YOU DO:

1. Preheat the oven to 325°F.

2. In the large bowl, mix together the flour, baking powder, baking soda, salt, cinnamon, nutmeg, and sugar.

3. With the spoon, make a well in the center of the mixture and add the vegetable oil and eggs.

4. Blend until just mixed.

5. Add the grated carrots and raisins, and stir.

6. Pour into greased muffin tins.

7. Bake 20 minutes.

WHILE YOU'RE WAITING

Panel 1: I'M FIXING YOUR DINNER RIGHT NOW..

Panel 2: WHILE YOU'RE WAITING, I THOUGHT YOU MIGHT LIKE SOME SOUP..AND WHILE YOU'RE WAITING FOR THE SOUP, I'LL BRING YOU SOME FRENCH BREAD..

7-23

Panel 3: AND WHILE YOU'RE WAITING FOR THE BREAD, I THOUGHT YOU MIGHT LIKE SOME CARROTS...

© 1988 United Feature Syndicate, Inc.

Panel 4: WHAT DO I EAT WHILE I'M WAITING FOR THE CARROTS?

(7-23-88)

While you're waiting for dinner to be ready,
try making and munching on these Veggie Bowls.

VEGGIE BOWLS

(makes 1 big bowl)

WHAT YOU NEED:

1 green, yellow, or red pepper, washed

1 celery stalk, washed

1 carrot, peeled

your favorite salad dressing

You'll also need a knife to slice the vegetables and
a spoon to scoop the seeds out of the pepper.

WHAT YOU DO:

1. Cut the pepper in half (straight through the middle, from top to bottom). Scoop out the seeds. Then cut one half into strips. The other half will be your bowl.

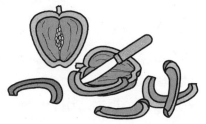

2. Cut the celery and carrot into sticks about four inches long each.

3. Put a little salad dressing in the bottom of your pepper bowl.

4. Stand the pepper strips and celery and carrot sticks up in the bowl.

5. Pull the veggies out and eat them one at a time.

6. Eat the pepper bowl!

LUCY'S GARDEN

(6-7-79)

It might be hard to grow an apple *bush* or potato *tree* (since they don't exist), but you *can* start your own vegetable garden.

WHAT YOU NEED:

a potato

a jar (with an opening
   bigger than the potato)

toothpicks

water

a windowsill

soil and a pot (optional)

WHAT YOU DO:

1. Pick a potato that is starting to sprout buds.

2. Pour some water into the bottom of the jar, and place the potato into the jar. You only want the bottom half of the potato (and the roots as they grow) to be in the water, so insert a few toothpicks into the potato and place them on the rim of the jar to keep the top of the potato from sitting in the water (so it won't rot!).

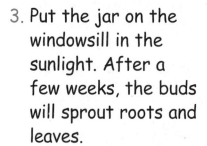

3. Put the jar on the windowsill in the sunlight. After a few weeks, the buds will sprout roots and leaves.

4. When the roots are about 1 inch long, you can plant your potato in a small pot with soil, or you can keep it in the jar and watch the roots get longer.

5. Enjoy your potato plant—just don't expect it to become a tree!

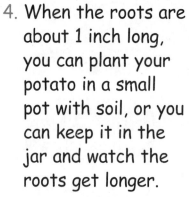

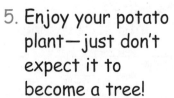

AN APPLE A DAY

(5-10-95)

Make a bag to carry your apples in—and use an apple to decorate it!

APPLE-STAMP FUN

WHAT YOU NEED:

newspaper

a canvas bag or a large
    piece of paper for your
    stamp drawing, instead

paintbrush

brown, green, and red
    fabric paint

2 apples

You'll also need a knife and an adult to help.

WHAT YOU DO:

1. Fold up some newspaper and put it inside the canvas bag so that your paint won't run all the way through to the other side. Lay the bag flat on a table or other hard surface. With the paintbrush, use brown paint to make a tree trunk on the bag. Let it dry.

2. Cut one apple in half horizontally. Then brush a thin layer of green paint onto the apple and press it onto the bag to stamp leaves onto the tree trunk. Repeat several times.

3. After the green paint dries, cut the other apple in half vertically. Brush red paint onto the apple and stamp red apples among the leaves on the tree.

4. Once the paint dries, fill up your bag with apples (or anything else you want to tote to school)!

TIP:. You can also use the apple stamps on paper, instead of on a canvas bag. But whatever you do, don't eat the apples after stamping!

DO YOU SEE THE STAR THE APPLE STAMP
MAKES IN THE MIDDLE OF THE GREEN LEAVES?

NOODLE ART

Snoopy lost his appetite because Woodstock made him think his spaghetti looks like worms, but it won't go to waste if he turns it into art!

WHAT YOU NEED:

a bowlful of cold, cooked spaghetti

black construction paper

a butter knife

waxed paper

WHAT YOU DO:

1. Arrange the spaghetti noodles on the construction paper in any design or shape you like. (The starch in the noodles make them stick to the paper.)

2. You can use a butter knife to cut the spaghetti, if you want different lengths.

3. To keep your masterpiece from squiggling around, cover it with a sheet of waxed paper and put a heavy book on top. Let it dry overnight.

PAINT A PIANO

Lucy's up to no good!

(6-11-68)

Okay, maybe you don't want to paint stripes on a piano, but you *can* make your own puffy paint with things you can find in your kitchen.

PUFFY PAINT

WHAT YOU NEED:

½ cup salt

½ cup flour

½ cup water

food coloring

empty squeeze bottle or plastic bag

You'll also need a large bowl, measuring cup, and a mixing spoon.

WHAT YOU DO:

1. In the bowl, mix together the salt, flour, and water (it should be the consistency of pudding).

2. Add food coloring, until you get the shade you want.

3. Transfer the paint to the squeeze bottle, or use a plastic bag (snip off one tiny corner at the bottom of the bag).

4. To decorate an object (like a box, or note cards, or even your backpack), slowly squeeze out your paint into any design you want. Try writing your name!

5. Let your project air-dry overnight.

84

FULL OF BEANS

(6-12-79)

Here's something else Lucy can do while she's waiting for her beans to grow.

BEAN MOSAICS

WHAT YOU NEED:

pencil   white glue

cardboard   assorted dried
                      beans and peas

paintbrush

WHAT YOU DO:

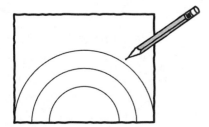

1. Sketch a design on
   the cardboard.

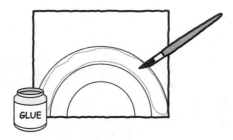

2. Use the paintbrush to cover a
   small portion of your design
   with a thick coat of white glue.

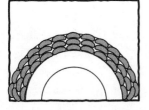 

3. Arrange one type or color
   of bean on top of the
   glued area.

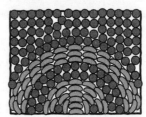

4. Continue painting on glue and
   placing beans, until the whole
   design is complete. Let your
   creation dry for several hours.

85

CEREAL MATH

(10-1-73)

Cold cereal? If you're like Peppermint Patty, you prefer a hot breakfast. But dry cereal can be fun to play with. Get your mind running at breakfast with this math activity.

Take a handful of multicolored cold cereal (like fruit rings). Look it over quickly and guess which color is most common.

GUESS: _____

Then arrange the cereal in rows according to color, creating a graph like the one below. This is called a bar graph, and it's a very useful way of recording how much there is of one thing compared to something else. Did you guess correctly? Eat the longest row first, with or without milk!

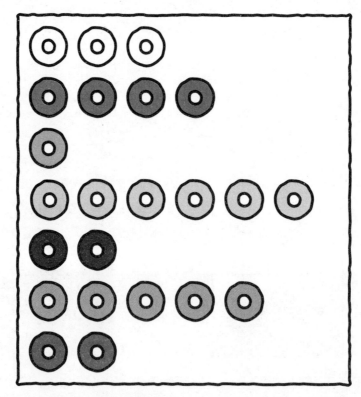

P.S. How else can you arrange the cereal, besides by color?

P.P.S. Why do you think Peppermint Patty was sleeping in Snoopy's doghouse?

PASTA PLAY

(12-26-60)

Here are two more fun party games for your next party
or the next time you get together with your friends.

SPEEDY SPAGHETTI

WHAT YOU NEED:

a strand of dried
   (uncooked) spaghetti
   for each player

a bowl of cereal rings
   (like cheerios or fruit
   rings) for each player

2 or more players

WHAT YOU DO:

1. Each player sticks a strand of spaghetti in her mouth.

2. Each player tries to collect as many cereal rings onto her stick of spaghetti as possible in one minute.

3. No hands allowed!

4. The player with the most cereal lined up on his spaghetti stick after one minute wins! Ready, set, go!

PEANUT PICK-UP STICKS

You can show off your skill with chopsticks when you play this game.

WHAT YOU NEED:

chopsticks for each player

a bowl for each player

a bag of peanuts (in their shell)

2 or more players

WHAT YOU DO:

1. Give each player a pair of chopsticks and an empty bowl. Spread the peanuts out on a table.

2. The players scramble to pick up as many peanuts as possible with their chopsticks and put them in their bowls.

3. When all the peanuts are off the table, the player who has the most peanuts in his bowl is the winner!

READY, SET, GO!

DON'T KNOW HOW TO USE CHOPSTICKS? CHECK OUT HOW:

1. Hold one chopstick between the tips of your fourth and third fingers and thumb, about $2/3$ of the length of the chopstick away from its tip. Hold the second chopstick like a pencil, between your pointer finger and third finger.

2. Hold the bottom chopstick still. Use your pointer finger to move the top chopstick up and down.

3. Practice holding onto the chopsticks and moving them until you feel comfortable. Then try picking up small objects, like peanuts and beans.

MARSHMALLOW MADNESS

Woodstock and his friends have decorated their sticks with marshmallows. You can make marshmallow artwork, too, and eat it when you're done!

WHAT YOU NEED:

a bag of large marshmallows and/or a bag of small marshmallows   pretzel sticks

WHAT YOU DO:

You can make all sorts of sculptures by attaching large and small marshmallows to pretzel sticks. And as long as you don't color the marshmallows with a marker, you can eat them when you're done.

Here are some sculpture ideas:

- ☐ Make marshmallow animals—can you make a marshmallow camel?

- ☐ Make a big marshmallow circle with big marshmallows and attach little ones

- ☐ Make a marshmallow pyramid or tree

- ☐ Be creative and have fun!

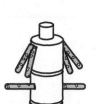

MARSHMALLOW SCARECROW

MARSHMALLOW ALIEN

MARSHMALLOW PYRAMID

MARSHMALLOW CAMEL

P.S. Check out the marshmallow snowperson on skis on pg. 61.

EAT YOUR ART

(11-27-67)

Maybe Lucy would appreciate Linus's artwork more if she could taste it. Use graham crackers instead of paper, and honey instead of glue, and you can create a beautiful piece of edible artwork!

WHAT YOU NEED:

honey

graham crackers

small paper cups filled with foods like raisins, chocolate chips, shredded carrots, apple slices, M&M's, gumdrops, colored cereal, peanuts, and gummy bears

You'll also need a butter knife.

WHAT YOU DO:

1. Spread a thin layer of honey over the surface of a graham cracker.

2. Use items from the cups to create a picture or a design.

3. Dig in!

PLAY CLAY

(2-7-59)

See if any dogs you know want to play catch with
the clay balls you can make with this recipe for clay.

WHAT YOU NEED:

1 cup flour	1 teaspoon vegetable oil
1 cup water	½ teaspoon cream of tartar
½ cup salt	food coloring

You'll also need a saucepan, a mixing spoon,
measuring cups and spoons, and an adult to help.

WHAT YOU DO:

1. Mix all of the ingredients together in the saucepan.

2. Add several drops of food coloring.

3. Cook over medium heat until the mixture begins to hold together.

4. Keep mixing so that the mixture doesn't stick to the sides of the pan.

5. Remove from the heat. When the clay is cool enough to touch, knead it until it's smooth.

6. This clay will keep for several weeks in an airtight container.

P.S. What else can you make with your play clay?

SMART STARTS

(4-26-84)

The next time you eat cereal, don't feel dumb like Charlie Brown.
Instead, do this smart activity to learn about volume
(that is, how much different containers can hold).

WHAT YOU NEED:

scissors   pan

sheet of construction paper   dry cereal

tape

1. Cut a piece of construction paper in half
   (so that each piece is the same size).

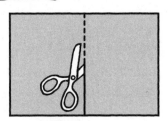

2. Tape each half into a tube—one a tall, skinny
   tube and the other a short, fat tube—and
   tape each tube so that it holds its shape.

3. Do both tubes hold the same amount
   (have the same volume)? To find out,
   stand the tubes up in a pan.

4. Fill one tube to the rim with
   dry cereal.

5. Now see if the same amount of dry
   cereal fills the other tube to the rim
   by emptying the cereal out of the first
   tube and transferring it to the second.

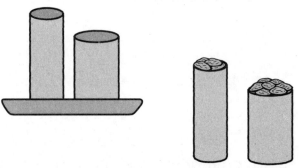

Even though they're different shapes, do the tubes have the same volume?
(Do they hold the same amount of cereal?)

DRINK A SNACK

(10-11-91)

There's nothing like a cookie with a glass of milk.
Try this recipe and you can have both in the same mouthful!

MILK-N-COOKIES MILKSHAKE

(serves 3)

WHAT YOU NEED:

4 scoops of vanilla ice cream	½ roll of store-bought cookie dough
5 cups milk	

You'll also need an ice cream scoop, a blender, and an adult to help you use it.

WHAT YOU DO:

1. Put the ice cream and milk in the blender.

2. Blend until smooth. Then add the cookie dough.

3. Blend again and serve.

WHERE'S THE WATERMELON?

A whole watermelon in your lunch?
No way! But how about watermelon in your lemonade?

WATERMELON LEMONADE

(serves 4)

WHAT YOU NEED:

6 cups watermelon, cubed and seeded

¼ cup raspberries

1 cup water

⅓ cup white sugar

½ cup lemon juice (4-5 fresh lemons)

You'll also need measuring cups and spoons, a blender, a mesh strainer, a pitcher, a large mixing spoon, and an adult to help you.

WHAT YOU DO:

1. Place the watermelon, raspberries, and water in a blender. Blend until smooth.

2. Pour the mixture through the mesh strainer into the pitcher.

3. Stir in the sugar and lemon juice until the sugar dissolves. Refrigerate until chilled.

SPLAT!

Something is always going wrong for Charlie Brown—especially when he's wearing a baseball glove!

(7-28-91)

Color this strip any way you like.

Do you think Charles Schulz ever drank baseball-flavored lemonade?

When it's too hot to stand in the outfield, try playing this game instead. You'll need four or more players.

1 Divide the players into two teams. The teams line up at opposite sides of a playing area. Decide which team will go first (flip a coin!).

2 The first team (Team 1) huddles together and secretly chooses two things—a place to be from (city, state, or country), and some action to perform (washing dishes, playing basketball, writing a story, etc.).

3 Team 1 then goes to the center of the playing area and says, "Here we come!" Team 2 asks, "Where from?"

4 Team 1 replies with the place they have chosen.

5 Team 2 asks, "What's your trade?" and the first team replies, "Lemonade!"

6 After they say "Lemonade," Team 1 begins to act out the action they chose earlier. Team 2 tries to guess what action Team 1 is performing.

7 When someone on the second team guesses correctly, a game of tag begins—Team 1 turns and tries to run back to their starting line, as Team 2 tries to catch them.

8 Whoever is caught on Team 1 joins Team 2 and the next round begins. This time, Team 2 picks the place and the action.

ACTION TIP:

When you are acting out your team's trade, have each team member perform a different step of the action. For example, if you are "making lemonade," one member can pick the lemons, one can squeeze them, and one can stir and sip.

SPECIAL TODAY

Wouldn't it be easier for Lucy to just sell lemonade?

(5-4-61)

Lemonade costs 50¢ a glass. Today it's on sale.
Which lemonade stand's special gives you the best price per glass?

SALE TODAY!
BUY ONE, GET ONE FREE!

SPECIAL SAVINGS!
HALF OFF REGULAR PRICE

NOW!
TWO FOR THE PRICE OF ONE

TODAY ONLY!
50% DISCOUNT

ON SALE!
SAVE 25¢ ON EVERY GLASS

(HINT: Is this a trick question?)

HOT CHOCOLATE

There is nothing like a good cup of hot chocolate on a cool fall day. See how many other words you can find in the letters of HOT CHOCOLATE. You can make words by using any letter squares that touch horizontally, vertically, or diagonally. List the words you find on the lines below. The list has been started for you.

H	O	T
C	H	O
C	O	L
A	T	E

LOT
_____   _____   _____

HOOT
_____   _____   _____

_____   _____   _____

_____   _____   _____

LAUGH OUT LOUD

(7-16-82)

WHAT DID THE ORANGE
SAY TO THE JUICER?

Give me a squeeze.

WHAT KIND OF GUM
DO ORANGES AND
LEMONS CHEW?

Juicy Fruit.

WHAT HAPPENS WHEN
A BANANA GETS A BAD
SUNBURN?

It starts to peel.

WHAT DO YOU GET WHEN
YOU CROSS AN ORANGE
WITH AN APPLE?

A perfect pear.

WHAT DO YOU GET WHEN
YOU CROSS A FRUIT WITH
A HORROR MOVIE?

Peaches and Scream.

Add your own fruity jokes here!

_____

_____

_____

_____

_____

_____

_____

_____

_____

_____

_____

_____

MAKE A SHAKE

Snoopy's brother would feel better fast if
Lucy made him this great shake. (And so would Linus!)

MONKEY SHAKE

(serves 2)

WHAT YOU NEED:

1 cup vanilla ice cream (about 4 scoops)

¼ cup milk

1 banana

4 tablespoons chocolate syrup

You'll also need an ice cream scoop, measuring cups and spoons, a blender, a knife to slice the banana, a couple of tall glasses, and an adult to help you.

WHAT YOU DO:

1. Put the ice cream and milk in the blender.

2. Peel and slice the banana, then add it to the blender, along with the chocolate syrup.

3. Blend until smooth. Pour in a glass, and serve!

COME AND GET IT!

It's like music to Snoopy's ears: Suppertime! Suppertime! Suppertime!

Match each caption to the correct strip.

> I STAY IN CLOSE COMMUNICATION WITH MY STOMACH

> I'VE NEVER SEEN ANYONE SO IMPATIENT

> ACTUALLY, IT LOOKED BETTER FROM A DISTANCE!

1.
(9-2-81)

2.
(12-29-84)

3.
(9-12-85)

102

YUM!

(6-12-66)

Yeah! It's suppertime!

What is your favorite supper?

What foods do *you* get excited about?

_____

_____

_____

_____

_____

_____

_____

_____

MIND YOUR MANNERS

(10-14-96)

Sally doesn't want to eat with Snoopy because she can't believe that he will have good table manners. Do your manners shine at suppertime or do you need a little help? Take this quiz to find out.

1 Dinner is ready. Your mom serves you the first piece of lasagna. It smells so good you can hardly wait! You:

    a) dig in. You don't want it to get cold.

    b) wait until everyone at the table has been served.

    c) take a taste when you think no one else is looking.

2 You're eating at a friend's house and the main course is broiled fish. You hate fish! You:

    a) say, "I'm not eating *that*!"

    b) take a tiny taste.

    c) hide it under your napkin.

3 It's Thanksgiving at Aunt Rose's. There are three forks set next to your plate. You have no idea which one to use when! You:

    a) wait to see which one your aunt uses.

    b) ask for help.

    c) start with the outside fork first.

4 You're saving the seat next to you at the lunch table for Brandy, but Amanda sits there instead. You:

    a) ignore Amanda and only talk to Brandy, who sits at the other end of the table.

    b) only talk to Amanda when she asks you questions.

    c) figure that you can sit with Brandy tomorrow, and enjoy Amanda's company today.

5 Halfway through lunch you notice that Tara has a poppy seed stuck between her teeth. You:

    a) catch her attention and motion with your hand to let her know.

    b) loudly say, "Hey Tara. You've got a poppy seed stuck in your teeth!"

    c) do nothing. You don't want to embarrass her.

6 You're eating dinner at Mama Roma's Italian Restaurant and you order a bowl of spaghetti and tomato sauce. You don't want to make a mess, so you:

    a) cut the spaghetti noodles into bite-sized pieces.

    b) twirl the spaghetti around your fork, using a soup spoon to twirl against.

    c) twirl the spaghetti around your fork, using the side of the bowl to twirl against.

7 Your grandparents are visiting, and tonight the whole family will eat in the dining room. The table is set beautifully. When you sit down, you:

    a) immediately take your napkin from the napkin ring and place it on your lap.

    b) wait for the food to be served and then place your napkin on your lap.

    c) tuck your napkin into the neckline of your shirt. You don't want to make a mess!

8 You've been invited to have dinner at your friend Ben's house. They are serving soup for a first course. There are two spoons to the right of your knife. You:

    a) use the smaller spoon. The larger one is too big to fit in your mouth.

    b) use the larger spoon at first, but the soup is so delicious that you pick up the bowl and drink the rest—you don't want to miss a drop!

    c) use the larger spoon, but only fill it up part of the way and sip quietly from the side of the spoon.

WORD PLAY

Just hearing the word "suppertime" makes Snoopy want to dance!

(6-19-69)

Here is a wacky way to write suppertime.
Can you figure out what foods these other wacky words are?
Write your answers in the blank boxes below each word picture.

SAMPLE:

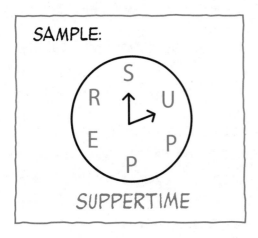

SUPPERTIME

LEFT
―――
PIZZA

1. [ ]

BAN/ANA

2. [ ]

6E6 66E

3. [ ]

```
 D CBA        B COP Q      D      P QW X
E                A            D    O   X
 FGH  I        Z     R      E    N  R  y
N     J          y    S    F   M  S    Z
 MLK          X WVU T      G  L T BA
                          H IJK  U
                              V
```

4. [ ]

SILLY SUPPER SENTENCES

"Silly Snoopy seems sad" is a silly sentence—all of the words begin with the same letter! Here are some more silly sentences. In each sentence, all of the blanks should be filled in with the same letter. Figure out the missing letter to complete each silly sentence. Then, try to say each sentence seven times fast!

1. __ete __icks at __izza.

2. __usan __ees __even __imple __oups.

3. __ice __ancy __ever __eeds __uts.

4. __our __airies __ound __rench __ries.

5. __enry __as __otdogs __alfway __ome.

HOW TO DRAW CHARLIE BROWN
FEEDING SNOOPY A SNACK

inspired by Charles Schulz

(5-3-70)

Day or night, Charlie Brown brings food out to Snoopy in his doghouse.
Follow these directions and you can draw this familiar scene.

1. To sketch a side view of Charlie Brown
   walking, start with a large circle for his
   head. Add a small circle for his ear. Make a
   rounded triangle for his body, with two ovals
   at the bottom for his feet. Sketch a circle
   for Charlie Brown's hand. In his hand, sketch
   Snoopy's rectangular-shaped dish. Now
   construct Snoopy's doghouse. Make two
   rectangular shapes: the one at the top is
   larger, with two of its sides angled.

2. Draw Snoopy on top of his house by starting with two circles for his head and snout and a smaller circle for his nose. Draw an overlapping oval for Snoopy's ear. To make his body, draw a teardrop shape. At the end of the teardrop shape, draw a long oval for his foot. Join Snoopy's head to his body by drawing a curved line.

3. Start to define Charlie Brown by drawing in his profile. Add his neck lines. Make his arms by drawing three lines holding Snoopy's bowl. Draw three lines to connect his body to his feet. Add a line for the bottom of his shirt. You can draw Snoopy's food in the bowl. (You decide what he's eating for dinner!)

4. Define your picture more by adding contour lines. Add Charlie Brown's hair, and add a collar, zigzag stripe, and sleeves to his shirt. Draw in his fingers holding the bowl. Add an extra line to Snoopy's house for the edge of the roof and angle the corners for dimension. Then draw in Snoopy's contour lines. Draw Snoopy's arm and paw at his side, a spot on his back, and his tail in the air.

5. Erase any sketch lines. Draw details like Charlie Brown's shoe laces, and color in his clothes. Add details to Snoopy's food, food dish, and doghouse. Draw grass by using bouncy lines.

FOOD FOOLERY

You can't fool Snoopy's stomach. He always knows when it's time to eat!

SPEAKING OF TIME:

1. Do you flavor your food with *time* or *thyme*?

2. Do you *peel* a banana or *peal* it?

3. Do you bite into a *pair* or a *pear*?

4. Do you bake cookies with *flour* or *flower*?

5. Do you get honey from a *be* or a *bee*?

6. Do you drink a cup of *tee* or *tea*?

Words like this—that sound the same, but are spelled differently and have different meanings—are called *homonyms*. Circle the homonym that fits correctly in each of the sentences above. Can you think of any other homonyms?

PENNY TOSS

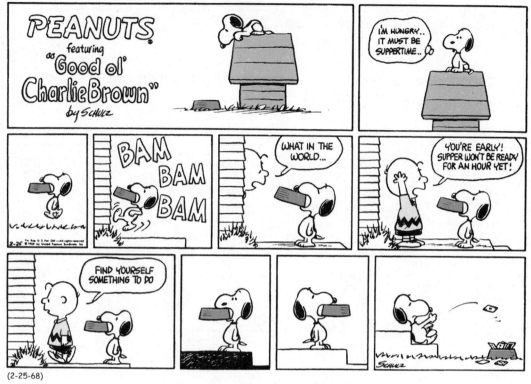

You can toss cards into an empty dish like Snoopy does,
or, you can try this fun tossing game.

WHAT YOU NEED:

black marker

an empty 12-cup egg carton

measuring tape

string (or another long and narrow object)

10-20 pennies

2 or more players

WHAT YOU DO:

1. Write the numbers 1 through 12, one number on each cup, on the inside bottom of the egg carton.

2. Place the carton on the floor. With the measuring tape, measure a line about five feet away from the carton, and mark it with a piece of string or anything else that's long and narrow.

3. The first player stands behind the line and tosses the pennies one by one into the carton.

4. When all of the the first player's pennies have been tossed, add up her points. (If three pennies land in the cup marked with number 1, you get three points. If five pennies land in the 10 cup, you get 50 points).

5. Now it's the next player's turn. Repeat steps 3 and 4.

6. The player with the most points wins.

NEW DISH

Snoopy needs a new dish. And another. And another!

The strips in each row are out of order. Unscramble them by writing the order in which they should appear in the little boxes.

1.

(9-23-97)

2.

(9-25-97)

3.

(9-24-97)

112

PUPPY PATH

(2-17-61)

Guide Snoopy to his supper by following the path of dishes.
You can move vertically, horizontally, and diagonally.

START

FINISH

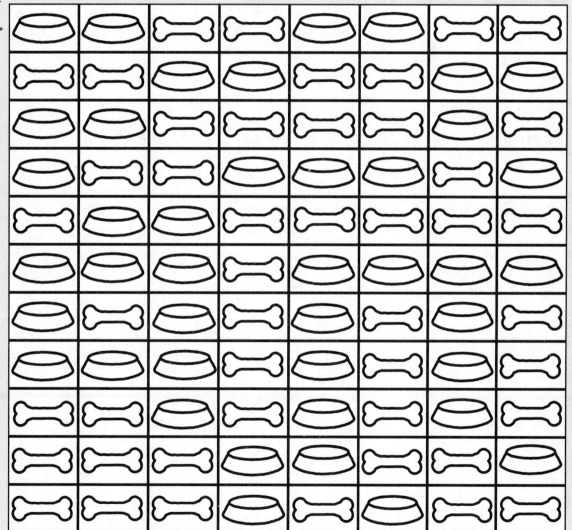

LEFT, RIGHT, UPSIDE, AND DOWN
inspired by Charles Schulz

In this strip, Snoopy is sledding down a hill in his supper dish. Charles Schulz drew Snoopy from the front, back, side, and even upside down.
See if you can draw Snoopy in the strip yourself.

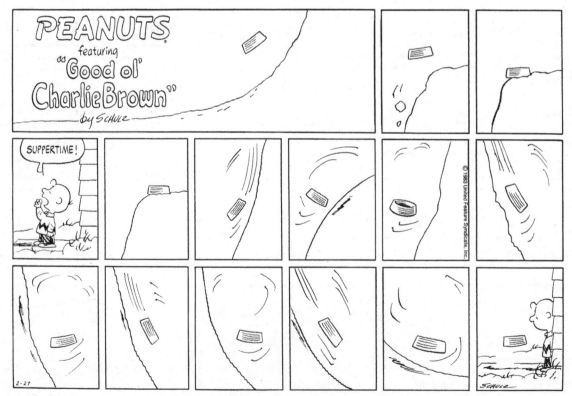

SHARE AND SHARE ALIKE

(6-10-99)

Some of the words in the captions are missing. Can you figure out each missing word and where it belongs, using the word box below? Write each correct word on its corresponding line below and then add it to the caption.

1. WHERE'D YOU GET THE _____?

2. IN THE _____.

3. I THINK YOU SHOULD ALWAYS SHARE WITH YOUR _____.

4. I _____. ALWAYS.

5. BUT NOT _____ TIME.

WORD BOX

SISTER	CAKE
EVERY	AGREE
KITCHEN	

HELP WANTED

FOR DESSERT TONIGHT WE HAVE CHOCOLATE CAKE..

BUT I KNOW A GOOD GUARD DOG WOULD NEVER EAT CHOCOLATE CAKE..

HOW ABOUT A WORTHLESS GUARD DOG ?

(12-29-92)

Can you think of a few other funny punch line captions for this strip? Write them in the blank bubbles below.

WHERE ARE THE CHIPS?

What does Charlie Brown say in the last caption? To find out, first fill in the answers to the clues below, one letter on each blank. Then transfer the letters to the matching numbers in the boxes below.

1. a baked fruit dessert with a crust on bottom and a crust on top

    ___ ___ ___
    12 17 18

2. a person who prepares food in a restaurant

    ___ ___ ___ ___
    13 14 15 16

3. the opposite of cold

    ___ ___ ___
    2 3 8

4. a kind of soda, coca-_____

    ___ ___ ___ ___
    4 5 6 7

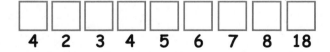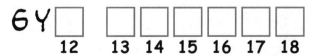

When you feel "gypped" (or something is a "gyp"), it means you feel like someone has cheated you. That is to say, you got less than you were expecting.

TOO MANY CHOICES

(10-12-86)

What kind of ice-cream eater is Sally? To find out, choose flavors from the word box to write in the blank boxes. Then, starting on the first line and going in order, line by line, take the letters that appear in the circles and write them in the spaces below.

WORD BOX

COOKIE DOUGH

STRAWBERRY

VANILLA

PISTACHIO

MINT CHIP

1. ⭘□□□□□□□□

2. □□□⭘□□□

3. □□□□⭘□□□

4. □□□⭘□□ □□□□□

5. □□□□□□□□□⭘

SALLY IS A □□□□□ ICE-CREAM EATER.

COOKIE CRAVINGS

Match each caption to the correct strip.

SOMETIMES I WISH I DIDN'T HAVE THIS AWESOME ABILITY	I'LL HAVE TO TEACH THOSE GUYS TO WHISPER
I COULD HAVE SWORN I HEARD A CHOCOLATE CHIP COOKIE CALLING ME...	YOU THOUGHT YOU HEARD A CHOCOLATE CHIP COOKIE CALLING YOU, DIDN'T YOU?

1.
(8-29-81)

2.
(9-23-81)

3.
(7-21-82)

4.
(7-22-82)

WHAT COULD BE BETTER?

(2-9-89)

Charlie Brown is trying to convince Snoopy that there's more to life than chocolate chip cookies. Can you help Charlie Brown by adding more things to the list? What do you think is more important than chocolate chip cookies?

CHARLIE BROWN'S LIST	YOUR LIST
Sunrises	
Sunsets	
Dancing	
Birthday Parties	
Holding Hands	
Cool Water	
New Shoes	

ICE CREAM! YOU SCREAM!

Have you met Eudora yet? She is one of Sally's classmates.

It's never too late at night for pizza and a sundae!
Use this recipe to make your own ice cream, and you'll be
ready for a marshmallow sundae anytime!

INSTANT ICE CREAM

(makes 2 servings)

WHAT YOU NEED:

1 cup whole milk	12 ice cubes
1 tablespoon sugar	2 tablespoons table salt
1 teaspoon vanilla extract	

You'll also need a a small resealable plastic bag, measuring cups and spoons,
a large resealable plastic bag, and marshmallows for topping.

WHAT YOU DO:

1. Pour the milk into the small bag. Add the sugar and the vanilla extract and seal the bag.

2. Place the ice cubes in the large bag and sprinkle them with the salt.

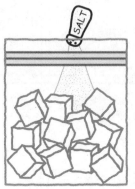

3. Put the small bag into the large bag and seal the large bag.

4. Shake the bag vigorously (get some friends to take turns) for a while. In about 10 minutes, the mixture will begin to thicken. Keep shaking. Soon it will look and feel like soft ice cream.

5. Pour the milk and sugar mixture into a bowl, top with marshmallows to make a marshmallow sundae, and enjoy! You can also add whipped cream and a cherry on top.

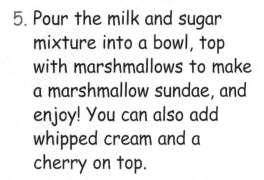

IN YOUR DREAMS

Snoopy isn't feeling well. Find out why...

(8-27-76)

Chocolate hamburgers! Do you love chocolate? If so, what other unusual chocolate foods can you dream up? Name them here.

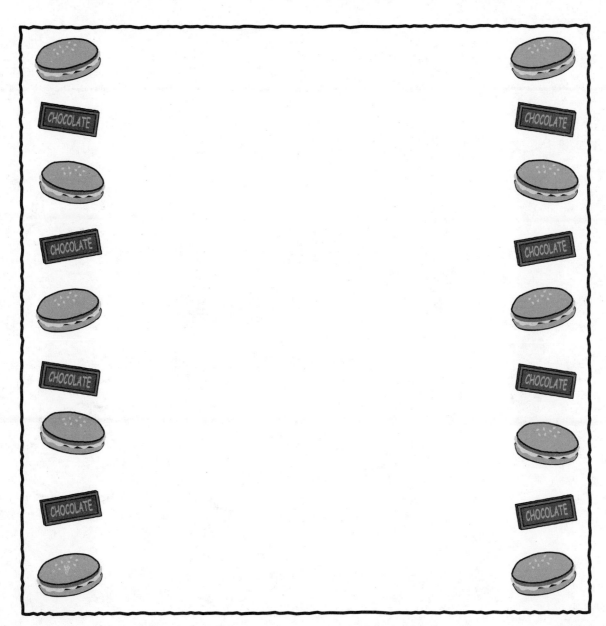

ICE CREAM CONES

(7-20-62)

Everyone loves ice cream, but not everyone likes the same cones! Read the sentences that follow. Then match each cone to the Peanuts character who eats it.

Sally wants vanilla on the bottom and chocolate on the top.

Charlie Brown doesn't like chocolate.

Linus wants three scoops.

Lucy only wants chocolate.

Snoopy will eat whichever cone is left.

124

UH OH!

Fill in the word balloons below with what you think
Rerun's thoughts are in each strip.

LEMON PIE AND CHOCOLATE CAKE

Snoopy sometimes pretends that he's a world famous surgeon, and he's full of advice about how to eat right (or at least how *he* should eat!). The strips below are out of order. Unscramble the four frames and place them in the correct order.

COMFORT FOOD

PEANUTS featuring "Good ol' CharlieBrown" by SCHULZ

No.1 CRAB

SLAM!

BOY, DO I FEEL CRABBY!

MAYBE I CAN BE OF HELP

WHY DON'T YOU JUST TAKE MY PLACE HERE IN FRONT OF THE TV WHILE I GO AND FIX YOU A NICE SNACK?

SOMETIMES WE ALL NEED A LITTLE PAMPERING TO HELP US FEEL BETTER...

© 1978 United Feature Syndicate, Inc.

4-23

SEE? I CAME RIGHT BACK! HERE'S A NICE SANDWICH FOR YOU, SOME CHOCOLATE CHIP COOKIES AND A COLD GLASS OF MILK...

NOW, IS THERE ANYTHING ELSE I CAN GET YOU?

IS THERE ANYTHING I HAVEN'T THOUGHT OF?

YES, THERE'S ONE THING THAT YOU HAVEN'T THOUGHT OF.....

I DON'T WANNA FEEL BETTER!!

(4-23-78)

What kind of foods do you like to eat when you're feeling sad or crabby?
How do you make your friends feel better when they're feeling low?

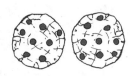

Do you ever wonder how Charles Schulz
came up with all his cartoon strip ideas?

"Nobody will believe this, but all the things that are said in the strip are things that I would normally say, and you would find out if you were around me for a week that this is just the way I talk all the time when I am with people that I know very well or with whom I feel comfortable." —Charles M. Schulz

COOKIES TO SMILE ABOUT

Panel 1: HERE, HAVE ANOTHER COOKIE...

Panel 2: WE HAD A GOOD TIME TODAY, DIDN'T WE? HAVE I MADE YOU HAPPY?

Panel 3: I'D SAY I'M ABOUT ONE COOKIE AWAY FROM BEING HAPPY..

© 1989 United Feature Syndicate, Inc.

(11-6-89)

See if you're as happy as Snoopy is when you eat one of these cookies.

SNOOPY'S HAPPY COOKIES

(makes 15 giant cookies)

WHAT YOU NEED:

$2\frac{1}{4}$ cups flour

$\frac{3}{4}$ teaspoon baking powder

$\frac{1}{2}$ teaspoon salt

1 cup butter, softened

$\frac{3}{4}$ cup white sugar

$\frac{1}{2}$ cup brown sugar

2 eggs

2 teaspoons vanilla extract

2 cups semisweet chocolate chips

You'll also need measuring cups and spoons, a medium bowl, a large bowl, a mixing spoon, a greased cookie sheet, and an adult to help.

WHAT YOU DO:

1. Preheat the oven to 300°F.

2. Mix the flour, baking powder, and salt together in the medium bowl.

3. Cream the butter (that is, mix it a lot!) and two kinds of sugar in the large bowl. Add the eggs and the vanilla extract. Mix well.

4. Gradually add the flour mixture in the medium bowl to the butter mixture in the large bowl and stir until combined.

5. Add the chocolate chips and stir again.

6. Using a small measuring cup, drop balls of cookie dough onto the greased cookie sheet. Leave 3 inches between cookies.

7. Bake for 30-35 minutes, until the cookies are brown.

8. Remove the cookies from the oven and let them cool.

HERE ARE SOME OTHER IDEAS FOR YOUR HAPPY COOKIES:

- Use M&M's instead of chocolate chips.
- Add 1 cup nuts.
- Put a scoop of ice cream between two cookies.
- Try other chips, like butterscotch, white chocolate, or peanut butter.
- Substitute 1/4 cup peanut butter for 1/4 cup of the butter in the recipe.

WHAT'S MY FORTUNE?

You can make your own fortune cookies!

FORTUNE COOKIES

(makes 24 cookies)

WHAT YOU NEED:

24 tiny strips of paper

butter to grease the cookie sheet

1 cup flour

$1/2$ cup sugar

3 tablespoons cornstarch

pinch of salt

4 egg whites (keep 1 egg white separated)

$1/2$ cup vegetable oil

3 tablespoons water

$1/2$ teaspoon lemon extract

You'll also need a pen, a cookie sheet, a large bowl, measuring cups and spoons, a medium bowl, a mixing spoon, a whisk, a spatula, a pastry brush, and an adult to help you.

WHAT YOU DO:

1. Write fortunes on the tiny strips of paper (look at the next page for some ideas).

2. Preheat the oven to 300°F and lightly grease a cookie sheet.

3. In the large bowl, mix together the flour, sugar, cornstarch, and salt.

4. In the medium bowl, mix together 3 egg whites and the vegetable oil.

5. Add the egg mixture in the medium bowl to the dry ingredients in the large bowl, and stir until smooth.

> You'll Be Lucky In Life

> There's Trouble Ahead

6. Add the water and the lemon extract. Stir again.

7. Drop six spoonfuls of batter onto the cookie sheet. The batter will spread into circles as it bakes.

8. Bake the cookies for about 10 minutes. While the cookies are baking, beat the last egg white with the whisk until it is white and foamy. You'll use it for glue.

9. When the cookies turn a light golden brown, take them out of the oven. Working quickly (so the cookies don't get hard), flip the cookies over on the warm cookie sheet with the spatula. Place a fortune in the middle of each cookie. With the pastry brush, spread a little egg white glue around the edges and gently fold the cookie in half. Hold the cookies closed until the two sides stick together. Then pinch the corners together.

10. Repeat with the rest of the batter until you have made 24 cookies.

Here are some ideas for your fortunes. Use these, or make up your own!

- You'll be very lucky in life.
- You'll have a fight with a friend.
- Money is coming your way.
- You'll get an "A" on your next test.
- You'll have the best teacher in school next year.
- You'll soon have a bad hair day.
- You watch too much television.
- You want a new pet.
- You eat too many cookies.
- Somebody loves you.
- You'll be happy today.
- You'll have trouble making a decision.
- You'll get a surprise in the mail.
- You'll go on an exciting voyage.
- Your wishes will come true.

CAMPFIRE COOK

(6-10-81)

Hot dogs and marshmallows? Maybe.
But how about bananas and marshmallows?
Try it and see.

BANANA BOAT

(serves 1)

WHAT YOU NEED:

1 banana (for each person)   chocolate chips

mini marshmallows

You'll also need a knife, aluminum foil, and an adult to help you.

WHAT YOU DO:

1. Peel the banana down one side (keep the peel on) and cut a wedge into it.

2. Place a few marshmallows and chocolate chips in the wedge.

3. Pull the peel back up and wrap the banana with aluminum foil.

4. Put the wrapped banana directly onto the coals of your grill or campfire (or in the oven if you're inside) for about five minutes.

5. Carefully remove, let cool, unwrap, and enjoy!

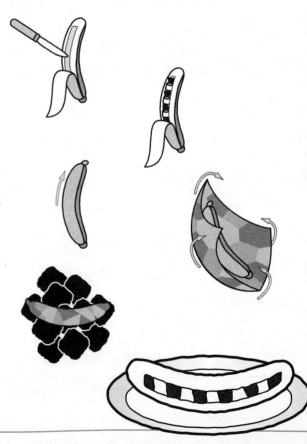

ON YOUR HEAD

(1-4-96)

Snoopy has trouble reading the menu when it's upside down. Do you think you can write upside down? First try writing your name. Then try writing anything you want! The upside-down alphabet will help you.

When you're done, turn the page around and check to see if you made any mistakes.

Z ⅄ X M Λ ∩ ⊥ S R

Q d O N W ⅂ ⋊ ſ

I H ⅁ Ⅎ Ǝ D Ɔ ᗺ ∀

_____

_____

_____

_____

FRENCH FOOD

(7-23-84)

Peppermint Patty is learning to speak French.

How about you?

Use the code to fill in the boxes below to learn in English
what Peppermint Patty said in French.

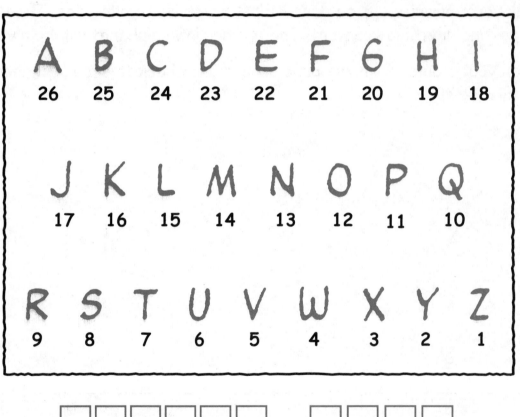

A	B	C	D	E	F	G	H	I
26	25	24	23	22	21	20	19	18

J	K	L	M	N	O	P	Q
17	16	15	14	13	12	11	10

R	S	T	U	V	W	X	Y	Z
9	8	7	6	5	4	3	2	1

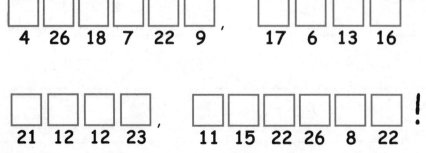

☐ ☐ ☐ ☐ ☐ ☐ ,   ☐ ☐ ☐ ☐
4 26 18 7 22 9   17 6 13 16

☐ ☐ ☐ ☐ ,   ☐ ☐ ☐ ☐ ☐ ☐ !
21 12 12 23   11 15 22 26 8 22

MENU MATH

Read this menu and answer the questions.

You have $5.00 to spend.

Choose three foods to order.

What will you order?

How much money will you have left over?

Hamburger	$3.00	Giant Cookie	$1.00
Hot Dog	$2.50	French Fries	$1.00
Mac and Cheese	$4.00	Milk Shake	$1.00
Spaghetti	$3.00	Fruit Juice	$ .50
Fresh Fruit	$1.50	Milk	$ .50

FOOD ORDERED   PRICE

_____ $ _____

_____ $ _____

_____ $ _____

Total: $ _____

Money left over: $ _____

DINER LINGO

(11-13-94)

If Peppermint Patty were ordering a fish sandwich at a diner, the waitress might call out to the chef: "one swimming loaf!" See if you can match the diner lingo to the real food names.

MOO JUICE	HOT DOG
BOWL OF RED	CHOCOLATE MILK
HOUSE BOAT	MILK
BOW WOW	DOUGHNUTS
VERMONT	CHILI
POPEYE	MAPLE SYRUP
LIFE PRESERVERS	SPINACH
MATS	LETTUCE
BLACK COW	PANCAKES
RABBIT FOOD	BANANA SPLIT

Redundant means using repetitive words to describe what you want to say. Since *tuna* is a *fish*, it's redundant to say both words.
What Peppermint Patty *should* have said is "I'll have a *tuna* sandwich!"

WAITING GAMES

While you're waiting to eat when you're in a restaurant,
try playing these fun games.

WHAT'S MISSING?

WHAT YOU NEED:

6-10 small objects, like a pen, a sugar packet, a coin, and a salt shaker

1 cloth or paper napkin

2 or more players

WHAT YOU DO:

1. One player, who is the leader, shows the other players all of the objects and names them.

2. Then the leader covers the objects with the napkin.

3. The leader reaches under the napkin and secretly removes one object (everyone else has to close their eyes).

4. The leader takes off the napkin. The other players have to guess what's missing.

5. Whoever is the first to guess correctly gets to be the leader next time.

DOTS

(for 2 players)

1. Make a square out of dots like the one below.

2. Take turns drawing lines to connect any two dots. The goal is to complete a box by drawing the fourth line. When you do, write your initials in the box.

3. Whoever completes the most boxes is the winner.

Play the game on this page now and then draw dots of your own the next time you are in a restaurant!

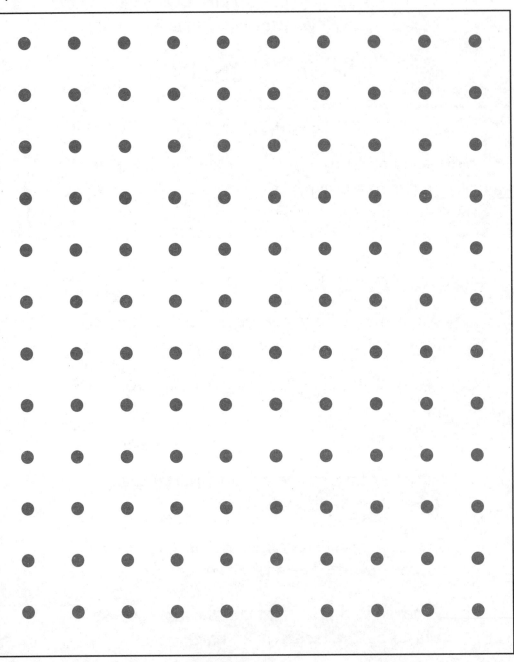

HA HA

A MAN GOES INTO A RESTAURANT, SEE, AND HE ASKS THE MANAGER, "WHY ARE ALL YOUR WAITRESSES SO SHORT?"

THE MANAGER SAYS, "SO IT'LL MAKE OUR ROOM LOOK BIGGER!" HA HA HA HA HA HA!!

I HATE RESTAURANT JOKES..

BONK

(8-10-88)

© 1988 United Feature Syndicate, Inc.

Snoopy doesn't like restaurant jokes. But you'll probably like these...

HAVE YOU HEARD ABOUT THE RESTAURANT ON THE MOON?

Great food, no atmosphere!

WHAT DOES A SKELETON ORDER AT A RESTAURANT?

Spare ribs.

WHEN KING KONG GOES OUT FOR DINNER, WHAT DOES HE EAT?

The restaurant.

WAITER, I'D LIKE A CUP OF COFFEE, PLEASE, WITH NO CREAM.

I'm sorry, sir, but we're out of cream. How about with no milk?

WAITER, I CAN'T SEEM TO FIND ANY OYSTERS IN THIS OYSTER SOUP.

Would you expect to find angels in an angel cake?

WAITER, WHAT'S THIS FLY DOING IN MY SOUP?

Um, looks like the backstroke to me, sir...

WAITER, THERE'S A FLY IN MY SOUP!

Keep it down sir, or they'll all be wanting one.

WAITER, THERE'S A DEAD FLY IN MY SOUP!

Yes sir. It's the hot water that kills them.

WAITER, WILL MY HAMBURGER BE LONG?

No sir, it will be round!

WAITER, DO YOU SERVE CRABS?

Sit down, sir, we serve anyone.

WE GO TOGETHER

(6-23-70)

Snoopy and Woodstock, Charlie Brown and Linus, Peppermint Patty and Marcie. These pairs often appear together in the Peanuts comic strips. Draw lines to match the foods that go together.

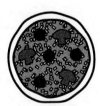

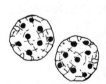

SPAGHETTI	EGGS
PEAS	PEPPERONI
PEANUT BUTTER	CREAM CHEESE
PANCAKES	SOUR CREAM
MEAT LOAF	CARROTS
HAMBURGER	MUSTARD
POTATO CHIPS	SYRUP
HOT CHOCOLATE	JELLY
BAGEL	MARSHMALLOWS
MACARONI	COOKIES
BACON	FRENCH FRIES
BAKED POTATO	MASHED POTATOES
MILK	CHEESE
PIZZA	SALSA DIP
HOT DOG	MEATBALLS

DIVE RIGHT IN

(2-17-61)

Pizza, parties, picnics, peanut butter. As you know by now,
The Peanuts Gang loves snacking and suppertime.

If you didn't share their passions before you read this book,
you probably do now! So, why not dive right in?

MAKE A PIZZA.

THROW A PARTY.

TOAST A MARSHMALLOW.

PLAN A PICNIC.

JUST MAKE SURE, UNLIKE SNOOPY,
THAT YOU LOOK BEFORE YOU JUMP!

HAVE FUN!

Pages 6-7: PIZZA WITH ALL THE TOPPINGS

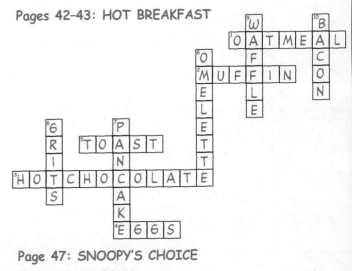

SHE CAN DEFINITELY MAKE A LOT OF DOUGH

Page 8: HAVE A SLICE!

2 slices for a 4-slice pie

4 slices for an 8-slice pie

6 slices for a 12-slice pie

3 slices for a 6-slice pie

5 slices for a 10-slice pie

7 slices for a 14-slice pie

BONUS: None of them—all the pizza pies are the same size, no matter how many slices they have!

Page 14: PIZZA MATH

40 slices

Page 15: RAINY PIZZA DAYS

IT TENDS TO COOL YOUR PIZZA DOWN

Pages 16-17: COLORFUL EXPRESSIONS

1. c	3. a	5. c	7. a	9. c
2. c	4. b	6. b	8. b	10. a

Pages 18-19: DOUBLE Z's MARK THE SPOT

Page 20: PIZZA TO THE RESCUE

1-WHAT'S THE NUMBER OF "VILLELLA'S TAKE-OUT PIZZA PARLOR"?

2-SAVED BY A PIZZA!

3-YOU WERE ROBBED!

4-I ALREADY ATE THE PIZZA...

Page 21: MATH MUNCHIES

200 pizzas   40 pizzas   20 pizzas   80 pizzas

Page 23: COMBINATION FUN

2	5	5	9
8	9	2	5
5	8	9	2
2	9	8	8

Pages 28-29: FORGET THE PARTY

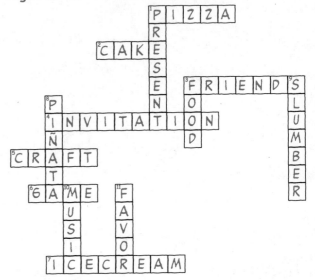

Page 30: SURPRISE!

WELL, I'LL BE A BROWN-EYED BEAGLE!

Pages 42-43: HOT BREAKFAST

Page 47: SNOOPY'S CHOICE

ENGLISH MUFFIN

Page 57: ARACHIBUTYROPHOBIA?!?!

1–WHEN YOU'RE REALLY LONELY THE PEANUT BUTTER STICKS TO THE ROOF OF YOUR MOUTH...

2–THIS IS THE FEAR OF PEANUT BUTTER STICKING TO THE ROOF OF YOUR MOUTH, AND MAY BE A BEAUTIFUL EXCUSE FOR NOT GOING TO SCHOOL SOME DAY...

Page 65: THE JOY OF EATING

ANSWER: JUNK FOOD

Page 68: LOST LUNCH

DOUGHNUTS

Page 74: FRUIT SALAD MIX-UP

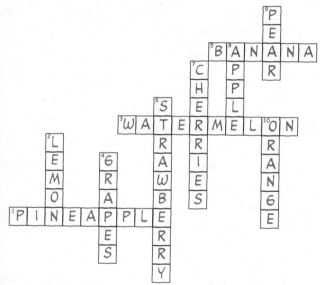

Page 75: BANANA BUNCH

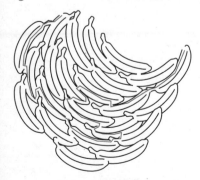

Page 98: SPECIAL TODAY

All the prices are the same — $.25 per glass.

Page 99: HOT CHOCOLATE

COT, ATE, LET, CAT, COAT, TO, TOO, HOT, TOOL, HOLE, COOL

Page 102: COME AND GET IT!

1–I'VE NEVER SEEN ANYONE SO IMPATIENT

2–I STAY IN CLOSE COMMUNICATION WITH MY STOMACH

3–ACTUALLY, IT LOOKED BETTER FROM A DISTANCE!

Pages 104–105: MIND YOUR MANNERS

1. b) It's not polite to eat until everyone at the table has been served.

2. b) If someone puts something on your plate, it's polite to give it a try. You never know, you may like it!

3. All answers are right. It's always okay to ask for help or observe others when you aren't sure what to do. But as a general rule, the silverware for the food that's served first is placed farthest away from the plate.

4. c) Don't be rude to a classmate. It's always better to be friendly to everyone. Who knows? Amanda may become your next best friend!

5. a) If you tell the whole table about the poppy seed, she will be embarrassed, but if you let her continue the meal with the poppy seed, she may be even more embarrassed! Try to let her know without shouting it to the rest of the world.

6. c) Although you may see grown-ups use a large spoon to help twirl their spaghetti, true Italians (and pasta lovers around the world) only need the side of the bowl as a twirling aid.

7. a) Your napkin goes into your lap as soon as you sit down and stays there for the whole meal. Never put it on the table. It should be left on your chair when you are done eating.

8. c) And please, no loud slurping sounds!

1. leftover pizza
2. banana split
3. scrambled eggs
4. alphabet soup

Page 106: WORD PLAY

Page 107: SILLY SUPPER SENTENCES

1. Pete picks at pizza.
2. Susan sees seven simple soups.
3. Nice Nancy never needs nuts.
4. Four fairies found french fries.
5. Henry has hotdogs halfway home.

Page 110: FOOD FOOLERY
1. thyme 2. peel 3. pear 4. flour 5. bee 6. tea

Page 112: NEW DISH

Page 113: PUPPY PATH

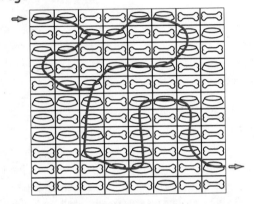

Page 115: SHARE AND SHARE ALIKE

Page 117: WHERE ARE THE CHIPS?
1. PIE 2. COOK 3. HOT 4. COLA

Answer:
CHOCOLATE GYP COOKIE

Page 118: TOO MANY CHOICES

1. PISTACHIO
2. VANILLA
3. MINT CHIP
4. COOKIE DOUGH
5. STRAWBERRY

Answer: Sally is a PICKY ice-cream eater.

Page 119: COOKIE CRAVINGS
1-SOMETIMES I WISH I DIDN'T HAVE THIS AWESOME ABILITY
2-YOU THOUGHT YOU HEARD A CHOCOLATE CHIP COOKIE CALLING YOU, DIDN'T YOU?
3-I COULD HAVE SWORN I HEARD A CHOCOLATE CHIP COOKIE CALLING ME
4-I'LL HAVE TO TEACH THOSE GUYS TO WHISPER

Page 124: ICE CREAM CONES

Page 126: LEMON PIE AND CHOCOLATE CAKE

Page 134: FRENCH FOOD

WAITER, JUNK FOOD, PLEASE!

Page 136: DINER LINGO

MOO JUICE—MILK
BOWL OF RED—CHILI
HOUSE BOAT—BANANA SPLIT
BOW WOW—HOT DOG
VERMONT—MAPLE SYRUP
POPEYE—SPINACH
LIFE PRESERVES—DOUGHNUTS
MATS—PANCAKES
BLACK COW—CHOCOLATE MILK
RABBIT FOOD—LETTUCE

Page 140: WE GO TOGETHER

SPAGHETTI—MEATBALLS
PEAS—CARROTS
PEANUT BUTTER—JELLY
PANCAKES—SYRUP
MEAT LOAF—MASHED POTATOES
HAMBURGER—FRENCH FRIES
CORN CHIP—SALSA DIP
HOT CHOCOLATE—MARSHMALLOWS
BAGEL—CREAM CHEESE
MACARONI—CHEESE
BACON—EGGS
BAKED POTATO-SOUR CREAM
MILK-COOKIES
PIZZA-PEPPERONI
HOT DOG-MUSTARD